Sarah Lawrey an

Cambridge IGCSE®
Computer Science
Coursebook

CAMBRIDGE
UNIVERSITY PRESS

University Printing House, Cambridge CB2 8BS, United Kingdom

One Liberty Plaza, 20th Floor, New York, NY 10006, USA

477 Williamstown Road, Port Melbourne, VIC 3207, Australia

314–321, 3rd Floor, Plot 3, Splendor Forum, Jasola District Centre, New Delhi – 110025, India

79 Anson Road, #06–04/06, Singapore 079906

Cambridge University Press is part of the University of Cambridge.

It furthers the University's mission by disseminating knowledge in the pursuit of education, learning and research at the highest international levels of excellence.

Information on this title: education.cambridge.org

First published 2015

20 19 18 17 16 15 14 13 12 11 10 9 8

Printed in Spain by GraphyCems

A catalogue record for this publication is available from the British Library

ISBN 978-1-107-51869-8 Paperback

Contents

Introduction

When we wrote this book we wanted to produce an information and creative resource that covered the latest IGCSE Computer Science syllabus. We wanted to make sure we covered all the syllabus elements, with as many real-life examples as we could include. We also wanted to add a couple of extension elements to demonstrate related areas that are just beyond this syllabus.

There is no programming language focus in this book. The aim of the programming section of the book is to provide a fundamental understanding the main programming concepts. These are developed through the use of pseudocode and flowcharts.

Examination

Examinations are likely to test your knowledge of topics from the architecture of computers and how they interpret data, to communication and internet technologies, and the ethical issues surrounding computers. They frequently also test your computational thinking skills independent of any programming language and ask you to construct designs for algorithms using the fundamental programming concepts.

To support your learning, each chapter has some sections to test your knowledge as you progress through the chapter, as well as exam-style questions at the end of each chapter.

We hope you enjoy developing your knowledge of Computer Science and gain a great understanding of the fundamentals of computational thinking. It is a vital skill that will be applicable to many areas of your daily life and give you the ability to be a great problem solver. After reading the book, we hope you become as passionate about Computer Science as we are.

How to use this book: a guided tour

Chapter – each chapter begins with a short list of the facts and concepts that are explained in it.

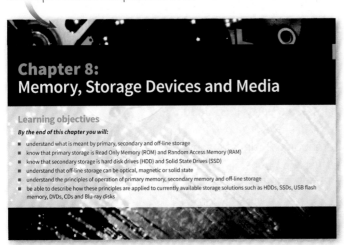

Chapter 8:
Memory, Storage Devices and Media

Learning objectives

By the end of this chapter you will:

- understand what is meant by primary, secondary and off-line storage
- know that primary storage is Read Only Memory (ROM) and Random Access Memory (RAM)
- know that secondary storage is hard disk drives (HDD) and Solid State Drives (SSD)
- understand that off-line storage can be optical, magnetic or solid state
- understand the principles of operation of primary memory, secondary memory and off-line storage
- be able to describe how these principles are applied to currently available storage solutions such as HDDs, SSDs, USB flash memory, DVDs, CDs and Blu-ray disks

Tip – quick suggestions to remind you about key facts and highlight important points.

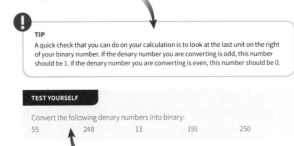

> **! TIP**
> A quick check that you can do on your calculation is to look at the last unit on the right of your binary number. If the denary number you are converting is odd, this number should be 1. If the denary number you are converting is even, this number should be 0.

TEST YOURSELF

Convert the following denary numbers into binary:

| 55 | 248 | 13 | 191 | 250 |

Test Yourself – exercises for you to test your knowledge and understanding.

Summary

- Data is valuable. It loses its value if it is lost, accidentally changed or corrupted.
- Computer security is the protection of computer systems and their data.
- Data can be lost accidentally through human error, theft, damage to equipment, power failure, hardware failure or misplacing portable media.
- Backups and verification help protect against accidental data loss. A backup is a copy of data, kept away from the computer system.
- Verification is a check which asks the user to confirm whether or not they wish to go ahead with an action.
- An unauthorised attempt to access a computer is known as an attack. As well as physical attacks (where the user has physical access to the computer), attacks can be made through the use of malware, phishing, pharming and Denial of Service (DoS).
- Malware is software that is designed to affect the normal operation of a computer. Malware comes in the form of viruses, worms, Trojan horses and spyware. Each form of malware can cause data loss or provide unauthorised access to data.
- Pharming is a technique which uses email to trick a user into giving away personal data.
- Phishing directs the user to a fake websites where they may inadvertently give away personal data.
- Denial of service attacks attempt to prevent access to data. A computer is used to overload a server with requests.
- Encryption is a technique that disguises the contents of a message using a key.
- Protocols are sets of rules that handle communication between computers.
- Secure Socket Layer (SSL) is a protocol that creates a secure, encrypted link between one computer and another. TLS is an updated, more secure version of SSL.

Exam-style questions

1. What is meant by data losing its value?
2. Explain what is meant by an automatic backup.
3. Explain how phishing and pharming trick a user into giving up personal data.
4. Explain how anti-virus software may help to prevent distributed denial of service attacks.
5. Explain why computer security is more effective when anti-virus software and firewalls are used.

Syllabus Check – links programming concepts explained in the text to the syllabus.

SYLLABUS CHECK

Convert positive denary integers into binary and positive binary integers into denary

> **🔑 KEY TERM**
>
> **Denary** – a system of numbers with a base of 10. Each unit used increases by the power of 10.
> **Binary** – a system of numbers with a base of 2. Each unit used increases by the power of 2.

Key Term – clear and straightforward explanations of the most important terms in each chapter.

Summary Checklist – at the end of each chapter to review what you have learned.

Exam-style Questions – Exam-style questions for you to test your knowledge and understanding at the end of each chapter.

Acknowledgements

The authors and publishers acknowledge the following sources of copyright material and are grateful for the permissions granted. While every effort has been made, it has not always been possible to identify the sources of all the material used, or to trace all copyright holders. If any omissions are brought to our notice, we will be happy to include the appropriate acknowledgements on reprinting.

Thanks to the following for permission to reproduce images:

p.7 wellphoto/Shutterstock; p.22 PeopleImages.com/Getty; p.28 alengo/Getty; p.28 nevarpp/Getty; p.31 Yagi Studio/Getty; p.32 Maciej Frolow/Getty; p. 32 Adam Gault/Getty; p. 33 JuSun/Getty; p.34 photovibes/Getty; p.36 123render/Getty; p.40 FRANCIS MILLER/Getty; p.47 Courtesy of International Business Machines Corporation, © International Business Machines Corporation; p.50 nikkytok/Shutterstock; p.50 CGinspiration/Getty; p. 66 Huchen Lu/Getty; p. 67 Stephen Krow/iStock; p.68 enterphoto/Getty; p.69 Tatiana Popova/Shutterstock; p.69 Aga_Rafi/Shutterstock; p.69 Neuratron; p.70 Mile Atanasov/Shutterstock; p.71 Photo courtesy of ION Audio (Ionaudio.com); p.72 Jack Hollingsworth/Getty; p.73 Christopher Dodge/Shutterstock; p.74 Marcus LindstrAm/Getty; p.74 Paul Bradbury/Getty; p.78 Denys Prykhodov/Shutterstock; p.79 Ricardo Saraiva/Shutterstock; p.80 shaunl/Getty; p.81 Monty Rakusen/Getty; p.82 Alex Kalmbach/Shutterstock; p.82 cveltri/iStock; p.87 lassedesignen/Fotolia; p.87 Juergen Faelchle/Shutterstock; p.88 BanksPhotos/Getty; p.89 Image Point Fr/Shutterstock; p.90 harpazo_hope/Getty; p.91 Ambrophoto/Shutterstock; p.99 Levent Konuk/Shutterstock; p.100 Andrey Artykov/Getty; p.101 daitoZen/Getty; p.104 William Andrew/Getty; p.106 PASIEKA/Getty; p.106 supergenijalac/Shutterstock; p.108 Ragnar Schmuck/Getty; p.109 CALC/Getty; p.112 Courtesy of International Business Machines Corporation, © International Business Machines Corporation; p.116 Michael Bodmann/Getty; p.116 Steve Outram/Getty; p.126 Sergey Nivens/Shutterstock; p.130 nevarpp/Getty; p.133 Derek Winchester/Getty; p.135 Undergroundarts.co.uk/ Shutterstock; p.136 ALFRED PASIEKA/SCIENCE PHOTO LIBRARY; p.137 Peshkova/Getty; p.144 marekuliasz/Shutterstock; p.145 Sam Burt Photography/Getty

Chapter 1:
Data Representation

Learning objectives

By the end of this chapter you will:

- understand how binary numbers are used by computer systems
- be able to convert to and from positive denary and binary numbers
- understand the use of hexadecimal notation
- be able to convert to and from positive denary and hexadecimal notation
- be able to convert to and from positive binary and hexadecimal notation
- understand how different types of data are stored as binary digits
- understand how data is compressed using lossy and lossless compression methods.

1.01 Binary number system

Data is information coded in a format ready for processing. Data is raw facts and figures and can be in the form of numbers, symbols or alphanumeric characters. As humans we use **analogue** data, such as sound or light waves and impulses on our skin. Everything we see and hear is a continuous transmission of analogue data to our senses. Analogue data is great for us as we can process and understand it. Computers cannot process analogue data, they are only capable of processing **digital** data. Any data that we want a computer to process must first be converted into digital data.

KEY TERM

Data – numbers, symbols or alphanumeric characters in their raw format before processing.

Analogue – this is the smooth stream of data that our senses process on a daily basis, such as a sound wave.

Digital – data represented in the values 1 and 0 that a computer can process.

TIP

Analogue data is data that is transmitted or received continually and it varies over a wide range. An example of analogue data is a sound wave. A sound wave is sent or received over a period of time and the frequency of the wave may differ greatly.

Digital data is data that consists of individually recognisable binary digits. A sound wave would be sampled at set time intervals and converted into a stream of binary digits.

Converting between denary and binary

KEY TERM

Denary – a system of numbers with a base of 10. Each unit used increases by the power of 10.

Binary – a system of numbers with a base of 2. Each unit used increases by the power of 2.

In our daily lives we use a **denary** number system. This system uses the digits 0–9 and it is called a base-10 number system. This means that the units it uses increase by the power of 10. If we take the denary number 123 we can calculate its value. Units begin at the right-hand side of the number and increase by powers of 10 as we move left.

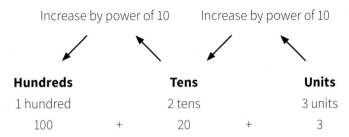

Figure 1.01 Denary number system

So we know the denary number 123 is one hundred and twenty-three.

Computers use a **binary** number system. This system uses the digits 0 and 1 and is called a base-2 number system. This means that the units it uses increase by the power of 2. The binary value represents the current flowing through a circuit: 1 means current is flowing, 0 means it is not.

If we take the binary number 1010 we can calculate its value as a denary number. Units begin at the right hand side and increase by the power of 2 as we move left. 1 indicates we use that unit, 0 indicates we do not.

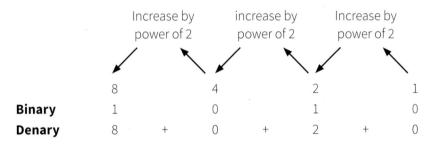

Figure 1.02 Converting a binary number into a denary number

So we know that the binary number 1010 as a denary number is 10.

When we are converting denary numbers to 8-bit binary, the units we use are 1, 2, 4, 8, 16, 32, 64 and 128. We indicate with a 1 or a 0 whether that number is required to create the denary number. For example, if we convert 150 denary to a binary number we could use the following steps:

1   Note down the binary units we can use from 128 down to 1, as in Table 1.01.

Table 1.01

128	64	32	16	8	4	2	1

2   Compare the denary number (150) to the first binary unit (128) and look to see if it is equal to or larger than it. 150 is larger than 128 so we do need 128 and a 1 can go beneath it (see Table 1.02). We can then deduct the 128 from 150 and we are left with 22.

Table 1.02

128	64	32	16	8	4	2	1
1							

3 Compare 22 to the next unit to the right (64) and look to see if it is equal to or larger than it. 22 is not larger than 64 so we do not need 64 and a 0 can go beneath it (see Table 1.03).

Table 1.03

128	64	32	16	8	4	2	1
1	0						

4 Compare 22 to the next unit to the right (32) and look to see if it is equal to or larger than it. 22 is not larger than 32 so we do not need 32 and a 0 can go beneath it (see Table 1.04).

Table 1.04

128	64	32	16	8	4	2	1
1	0	0					

5 Continue this process till you get to the end of the units and deduct the value of any unit that you use.

Table 1.05

128	64	32	16	8	4	2	1
1	0	0	1	0	1	1	0

So the denary number 150 is 10010110 as an 8-bit binary number (see Table 1.05).

If we calculate the denary number by adding together all the binary units that are used then the largest number we can make with eight binary bits is 255:

$$128 + 64 + 32 + 16 + 8 + 4 + 2 + 1 = 255$$

TIP

A quick check that you can do on your calculation is to look at the last unit on the right of your binary number. If the denary number you are converting is odd, this number should be 1. If the denary number you are converting is even, this number should be 0.

TEST YOURSELF

Convert the following denary numbers into binary:

55   248   13   191   250

To convert 8-bit binary numbers back into denary we need to add together all of the binary units that are marked as required by the digit 1. If we take the binary number 10010100 we can draw a table to see what units are needed:

Table 1.06

128	64	32	16	8	4	2	1
1	0	0	1	0	1	0	0

This means that the denary conversion of this binary number is:

$$128 + 16 + 4 = 148$$

You can use the quick check again to see if your denary number is correct, by using the rule that if the number to the far right in the binary number is 1, the denary number should be odd, otherwise it should be even.

Beyond 8-bit binary

We have looked at examples that convert 8-bit binary numbers into denary. We can easily apply the same principles to convert beyond eight bits, by simply using further binary units beyond 128. For example, the 12-bit binary number 101100101101 would be converted as shown in Table 1.07:

Table 1.07

2048	1024	512	256	128	64	32	16	8	4	2	1
1	0	1	1	0	0	1	0	1	1	0	1

$$2048 + 512 + 256 + 32 + 8 + 4 + 1 = 2861$$

The 16 bit binary number 1001100110011001 would be converted as shown in Table 1.08.

Table 1.08

32768	16384	8192	4096	2048	1024	512	256	128	64	32	16	8	4	2	1
1	0	0	1	1	0	0	1	1	0	0	1	1	0	0	1

$$32768 + 4096 + 2048 + 256 + 128 + 16 + 8 + 1 = 39321$$

Measuring memory size

Most computer systems have storage which is measured in bytes. A byte is a unit of data that is eight binary digits long. A byte can be used to represent a character, for example a letter, a number or a symbol. It can also hold a string of bits that can be used to build an image, for example.

Computer storage is usually measured in multiples of bytes. A byte is abbreviated with the capital letter 'B'. A bit is one eighth of a byte and is abbreviated with a lower-case 'b'. The measurements for storage are shown in Table 1.08.

Table 1.09

Unit of measurement	Abbreviation	Conversion
Byte	B	8 bits
Kilobyte	kB	1024 bytes
Megabyte	MB	1024 kB
Gigabyte	GB	1024 MB
Terabyte	TB	1024 GB

The conversion units are commonly rounded down to reflect the standard definition of the units of measurement. For example kilo means one thousand and mega means one million. Therefore they can be represented as shown in Table 1.09.

Table 1.10

Unit of measurement	Abbreviation	Conversion
Byte	B	8 bits
Kilobyte	kB	1000 bytes
Megabyte	MB	1000 kB
Gigabyte	GB	1000 MB
Terabyte	TB	1000 GB

Storage capacity is continuously growing and is now expanding beyond the terabyte into 1000 (1024) TB, known as the petabyte. However, the terabyte is ample for what most people require a computer for on a daily basis.

Using binary in computer registers

SYLLABUS CHECK

Use binary in computer registers for a given application (such as in robotics, digital instruments and counting systems).

KEY TERM

Register – small piece of memory where values can be held.

A **register** is a small piece of memory built into the central processing unit (CPU) of a computer system where values and instructions are temporarily held. It is not part of primary memory or secondary storage. Although they are small in capacity, registers have an extremely fast read and write rate, meaning data can be written to and read from a register much quicker than from primary memory or secondary storage. Therefore computer systems use registers to hold values and instructions for processing, to increase the speed at which they can be processed. If these values and instructions were processed straight from primary memory, processing would be much slower.

There are different types of register, such as processor registers and hardware registers. Processor registers, for example the program counter (PC), the accumulator and the memory address register (MAR), are used to process data. These registers are part of the CPU and can be written to and read from extremely quickly. The fast speed of access makes registers very suitable for situations where small amounts of data need to be accessed quickly, such as performing calculations.

Hardware registers are specific to different types of hardware and are used to convey a signal. Consider a robot arm that has various motors to perform different operations, for example, raise the arm, open the grip and close the grip. Each motor works via a signal, 1 for on, 0 for off. A register is used for each motor to convey the signal.

Figure 1.03 A robot arm uses hardware registers to control each motor. The register conveys the signal that turns the motor on or off

In a digital instrument, a register might be used to convey whether the device is sending a signal to the computer, 1 or 0. The instrument will have various registers to convey signals either way.

1.02 Hexadecimal number system

Hexadecimal is another number system that is used. Computers do not actually process hexadecimal, they convert it into binary before processing it. Programmers work with hexadecimal as it is easier for humans to read than binary. This is because it is a much shorter way of representing a byte of data, as reading and understanding lots of binary 1s and 0s can be difficult. In the same way, programs that are written in hexadecimal are easier to **debug** than those written in binary. Computers convert hexadecimal data into binary before processing it.

7

Hexadecimal – a system of numbers with a base of 16. Each unit used increases by the power of 16.

Debug – finding and fixing problems and errors in a program.

Hexadecimal (hex) is used as a notation for colour in HTML. Hex colour notations are normally six digits and each hex notation represents a different colour, for example #FFAA33 is orange and #000000 is black. In the hex code #FFAA33 the first two digits are the red component, the second two the green component and the last two the blue component. All three together create the colour orange.

FFFFFF	000000	333333	666666	999999	CCCCCC	CCCC99	9999CC	666699
660000	663300	996633	003300	003333	003399	000066	330066	660066
990000	993300	CC9900	006600	336666	0033FF	000099	660099	990066
CC0000	CC3300	FFCC00	009900	006666	0066FF	0000CC	663399	CC0099
FF0000	FF3300	FFFF00	00CC00	009999	0099FF	0000FF	9900CC	FF0099
CC3333	FF6600	FFFF33	00FF00	00CCCC	00CCFF	3366FF	9933FF	FF00FF
FF6666	FF6633	FFFF66	66FF66	66CCCC	00FFFF	3399FF	9966FF	FF66FF
FF9999	FF9966	FFFF99	99FF99	66FFCC	99FFFF	66CCFF	9999FF	FF99FF
FFCCCC	FFCC99	FFFFCC	CCFFCC	99FFCC	CCFFFF	99CCFF	CCCFF	FFCCFF

Figure 1.04 Hex colour codes

Standard Windows error message codes are given in hexadecimal notation, for example error code 404 (meaning 'File not found') is a hexadecimal notation.

HTTP Error 404

404 Not Found

The Web server cannot find the file or script you asked for.
Please check the URL to ensure that the path is correct.

Please contact the server's administrator if this problem persists.

Figure 1.05 404 error code

Media Access Control (MAC) addresses are 12-digit hexadecimal numbers that uniquely identify each different device in a network. An example of a MAC address would be 00-1B-63-84-45-E6. You can learn more about MAC addresses in Chapter 2.

Machine code consists of simple instructions that are directly executed by the CPU. Hexadecimal is used for machine code as each byte can be coded as two hexadecimal symbols. You can learn more about machine code in Chapter 3.

Represent integers as hexadecimal numbers.

Hexadecimal is a base-16 number system. This means that the units it uses increase by the power of 16.

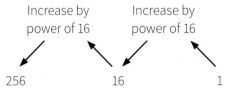

Increase by
power of 16

Increase by
power of 16

256   16   1

Figure 1.06 Hexadecimal base-16 number system

Hexadecimal uses 16 symbols, the numbers 0–9 and the letters A–F. The notation for each denary number between 0 and 15 is shown in Table 1.10.

Table 1.11

Denary	0	1	2	3	4	5	6	7	8	9	10	11	12	13	14	15
Hexadecimal	0	1	2	3	4	5	6	7	8	9	A	B	C	D	E	F

The reason for using the symbols A–F for the decimal numbers 10–15 is because only one symbol can be used per unit required in hexadecimal. For example, the denary number 10 has two symbols and hexadecimal only uses one symbol for each unit, so we use the letter 'A'. Similarly 14 has two symbols, so we use the letter 'E' instead. This means that we can use a single symbol for each unit. The same system applies in base ten: each unit is represented by one digit.

Converting between denary and hexadecimal

Convert positive hexadecimal integers to and from denary.

To convert the denary number 55 into hexadecimal we need to calculate how many of the unit 16 and how many of the unit 1 are required. As hexadecimal is a base-16 system it increases in unit by the power of 16. We can use up to fifteen 1s before we use a 16. We can then use up to a further fifteen 1s before we use the next 16.

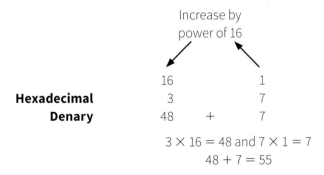

Increase by
power of 16

16   1

Hexadecimal   3   7
Denary   48   +   7

$3 \times 16 = 48$ and $7 \times 1 = 7$
$48 + 7 = 55$

Figure 1.07 Converting a denary number into hexadecimal

The denary number 55 in hexadecimal notation is 37. This means we use three 16s and seven 1s to create the denary number 55. If the denary number is larger than fifteen 16s (the largest amount of 16s that can be used) then we use the next unit in the base-16 system. If we were to convert the denary number 1080 into hexadecimal we do what is shown in Figure 1.08.

9

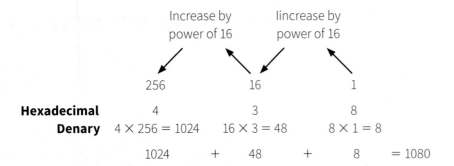

Figure 1.08 Hexadecimal notation for denary number 1080

Therefore the hexadecimal notation for the denary number 1080 is 438.

TEST YOURSELF

Convert the following denary numbers into hexadecimal:

101

1551

65

168

20

Convert the following hexadecimal notations into denary numbers:

15

1AB

E9

2F2

23

Converting between hexadecimal and binary

SYLLABUS CHECK

Convert positive hexadecimal integers to and from binary.

To convert binary into hexadecimal we take each binary number and separate it into 4-digit nibbles. If we take the binary number 1011 1100 1001 we would split it into three 4-digit nibbles, 1011, 1100 and 1001. We can then convert each nibble into a hexadecimal symbol. To do this we use the first four binary places 1, 2, 4 and 8 to calculate each hexadecimal symbol as shown in Figure 1.09.

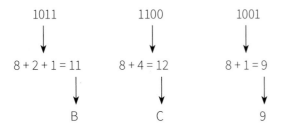

Figure 1.09 Converting a binary number into hexadecimal

Therefore 1011 1100 1001 in hexadecimal notation is BC9.

To convert hexadecimal notation back into binary we reverse the process. We take the hexadecimal notation BC9 and convert the denary value of each hexadecimal unit into a 4-bit binary number. We then join the binary numbers together:

Hexadecimal:	B	C	9
Denary:	11	12	9
Binary conversion:	1011	1100	1001

We can convert a 16 digit binary number in the same way. If we take the binary number 1001001110001010 we would split it into four 4-digit nibbles 1001, 0011, 1000 and 1010.

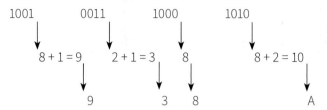

Figure 1.10 Converting a 16 digit binary number into hexadecimal

Therefore 1001001110001010 in hexadecimal notation is 938A.

TEST YOURSELF

Convert the following binary numbers into hexadecimal notations:

1010 1100   1100 1010

1101 1011 0111   0001 1111 0011

1001 1001 1000

1.03 Data storage

As computers can only process the 1s and 0s that we know to be binary, all data stored on a computer is in binary form. If we had to carry out our daily tasks on a computer using only binary it would be extremely time consuming and challenging.

Imagine having to write an email to your friends using only binary. Typing the 1s and 0s that represent each **character** would take you much longer than typing out the characters the binary numbers represent. Also, imagine having to type in each binary digit needed to create your favourite images – it would be extremely difficult. Depending on its resolution, a character might require 100 bits of data. An image might require millions of bits.

A number of systems and software were developed to do this for users and they help a computer store different data such as text, images, video and audio.

 KEY TERM

Character – text, numbers and symbols, for example each key on a keyboard.

Text, numbers and symbols

There are two systems commonly used for character (text, numbers and symbols) representation, namely ASCII and Unicode. ASCII uses only 8 bits, giving a possible 256 characters. It is suitable for Standard English but does not contain a large enough character set for some other languages. This is when Unicode is used as it contains many more characters. Unicode uses 16 bits, giving 65 536 possible characters. In ASCII and Unicode each character is represented as a binary number. For example, the letter A is 01000001.

In ASCII each character will take 1 byte of storage space as it is made up of 8 bits. In Unicode a character takes up 2 bytes as it is made up of 16 bits. Capital letters and small case letters have individual binary codes, as do numbers and punctuation.

The word 'Computer' would be as shown in Figure 1.11.

C – 01000011	u – 01110101	Computer =
o – 01101111	t – 01110100	01000011 01101111 01001101 01110000
m – 01001101	e – 01100101	01110101 01110100 01100101 01110010
p – 01110000	r – 01110010	

Figure 1.11 The word 'Computer' in ASCII

TEST YOURSELF

Search for an ASCII table on the internet and try and decode this message:
01000011011011111010011010101110000011101010111010001100101011100100101001101
10001101101001010001010110111001100011011001010110100101110011011001100111
01010110111000100001
Using the same ASCII table write a message for your friend to decode.

Pictures

We regularly use our computers to store and view images. An image as we see it is analogue data, but a computer will only understand it if it is digital data. We need to convert analogue data into digital data for a computer to process it. This can be done using various devices, such as a scanner or a digital camera.

Images are made up of pixels. A pixel is a tiny dot on the screen. If an image was simply black and white, each pixel would either be black or white. A 1 would represent a black pixel and a 0 would represent a white pixel. Using this we can look simply at how an image is created.

If we are given a series of binary data we can use this in a grid. We need to know the dimensions of the grid to be able to create the image. This data is called metadata. Metadata is what tells the computer how many pixels wide and how many pixels high an image should be. This is the 'resolution' of an image. The grid in Figure 1.12 is 11 × 12.

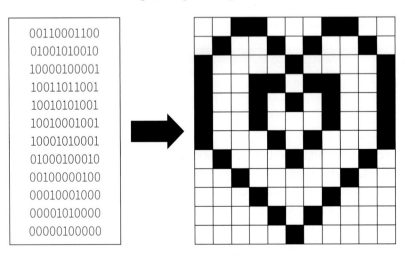

Figure 1.12 An image created using binary data

We have taken the binary data and created an image from it, a lovely heart! If we want an image to have more than just two colours, a computer needs further binary data to represent the colour of each pixel. Most colours are made up of red, green and blue in the RGB colour system. In this system the shade of each colour R, G and B will be represented in a byte for each. This is why images can become large files, especially when they are high in quality. To get the correct colour depth in each pixel to create a detailed image, the amount of binary data needed is much greater.

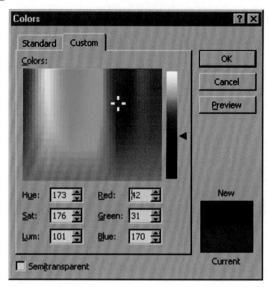

Figure 1.13 RGB colour scale

Sound

The sound we hear is also analogue but, as we know, computers work digitally and can only process binary. We need to convert the analogue sound into binary for a computer to be able to process it. Sound is recorded using a microphone and converted to binary by software.

Sound is recorded at set timed intervals; this process is known as sampling. The samples are then converted into binary. If the set timed intervals are closer together, the sound track will be higher in quality. Simply with more samples the sound can be more accurately captured.

Sample rates are measured in hertz. 1 hertz equals 1 sample per second. A telephone communication samples a voice at 8000Hz but a higher quality recording, such as a CD, samples music at 44 100Hz.

Take the simple sound wave in Figure 1.14.

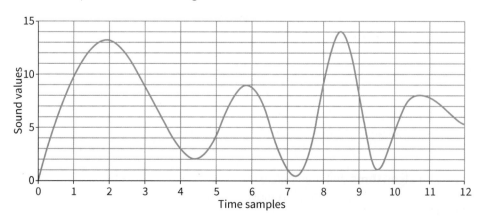

Figure 1.14 Sound wave

If we record the sound value at each time sample we would have the values in Table 1.11.

Table 1.12

Time sample	1	2	3	4	5	6	7	8	9	10	11	12
Sound value	9	13	9	3.5	4	9	1.5	9	8	5	8	5.5

If we then play back the recording the system will use the value at each sample interval to do this. The resultant wave is shown in Figure 1.15.

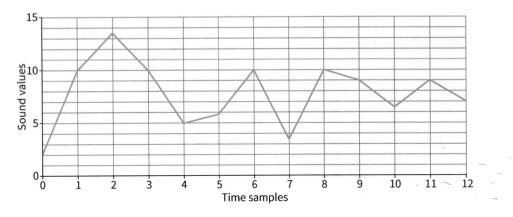

Figure 1.15 Sound wave created by playing back a recorded sound

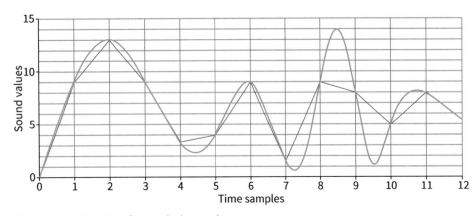

Figure 1.16 Quality of recorded sound

This is what affects the quality of recorded sound. The closer together the time samples that are taken, the higher the quality of the recorded sound. This is because when the sound is played back it has more data to help create a more accurate sound. If the time samples were closer together in Table 1.11, when the recorded sound is played back it may not miss so many of the peaks and troughs it has with the current time samples.

Data compression

Data compression is when the bit structure of a file is manipulated in such a way that the data in a file will become smaller in size. This means that less storage space will be needed to store the file and the file will be easier to transmit from one device to another.

Data compression is done by using compression **algorithms** that manipulate the data. These algorithms normally manipulate the data so that repeating data is removed, either on a temporary or a permanent basis, depending on the method used. You can learn more about algorithms in Chapter 13.

KEY TERM

Algorithm – a step-by-step set of instructions.

There are two main methods for compressing data: lossy and lossless.

SYLLABUS CHECK

Show understanding of the principles of data compression (lossless and lossy compression algorithms) applied to music/video, photos and text files.

Lossy compression

Lossy is derived from the word 'loss' and this refers to the way this method of compression works. With lossy compression, data that is deemed redundant or unnecessary is removed in the compression process. The data is removed permanently, so it is effectively 'lost'. This way the size of the file is reduced.

Lossy compression is mostly used for multimedia such as audio, video and image files. This is mostly done when streaming these files, as a file can be streamed much more effectively if it is smaller in size.

If a lossy compression method is used on a music file it will try to remove all background noise and noises that may not be heard by the human ear. This data isn't hugely necessary for playing the track; removing it will mean the track will not sound exactly as it did when recorded, but it will be a very close representation.

Lossless compression

Lossless refers to a method of compression that loses no data in the process. In lossless compression, the compressed data can be reversed to reconstruct the data file exactly as it was. Lossless compression is used when it is essential that no data is lost or discarded during the compression process. There are many different lossless compression algorithms; most work using a shorthand to store the data that can be then reconstructed when the file is opened.

If a lossless compression method is used on a music file it will not lose any of the data from the file. A possible way to compress the data would be to look for repeating patterns in the music. It would store this pattern once along with how many times it is repeated. This way repeating data is reduced. When the music track is played, the full track, exactly as it was recorded, can be reconstructed and listened to. People may use lossless compression when downloading a music track if they want the highest quality possible and to hear the track exactly as it was recorded. Lossless compression can also be used when storing text files.

Consider the following message:

**WHEN IT IS SNOWING HEAVILY LOOK OUTSIDE.
LOOK OUTSIDE IT IS SNOWING HEAVILY.**

Excluding the spaces between the words and the full stops, the message has a total of 62 characters. 1 character requires 1 byte of storage, so we would need 62 bytes of memory to store this message.

15

When we examine the message we can see that it consists of words that are mostly repeated. Instead of storing all 62 characters individually, we could instead store the words and the positions at which they occur in the message, in a lookup table:

Table 1.13

Word	Position(s) in the message
WHEN	1
IT	2 10
IS	3 11
SNOWING	4 12
HEAVILY	5 13
LOOK	6 8
OUTSIDE	7 9

When we store the message this time we need 1 byte for each character in each word and 1 byte for each position the word occurs in the message:

Table 1.14

Word	Position(s) in the message
WHEN	1
IT	2 10
IS	3 11
SNOWING	4 12
HEAVILY	5 13
LOOK	6 8
OUTSIDE	7 9
TOTAL BYTES: 33	TOTAL BYTES: 13

Therefore we would need 33 bytes to store the words and 13 bytes to store the positions, giving a total of 46 bytes. This is much less than the 62 bytes we required with our original method. No data has been lost and we have reduced our storage requirements by 26%, quite a saving! To recreate the message, the computer simply retrieves the words and places them in the positions allocated. We should note that the amount of compression we can achieve varies depending on the data we wish to store.

Consider a second message:

ASK NOT WHAT YOUR FRIEND CAN DO FOR YOU.
ASK WHAT YOU CAN DO FOR YOUR FRIEND.

Excluding spaces and full stops, this message has 59 characters, therefore requiring 59 bytes for storage. This message is shorter than that in our first example, which required 62 bytes. If we were to apply our lossless compression algorithm, we would end up with:

Table 1.15

Word	Position(s) in the message
ASK	1 10
NOT	2
WHAT	3 11
YOUR	4 16
FRIEND	5 17
CAN	6 13
DO	7 14
FOR	8 15
YOU	9 12
TOTAL BYTES: 31	**TOTAL BYTES: 17**

We need 31 bytes to store the words and 17 bytes to store the positions, giving a total of 48 bytes. This again is less than the 59 bytes required with our original method. This time we have reduced our storage requirements by a lesser amount though of 19%. This message, even though it was originally shorter than our first message, would after compression require more storage space than the first message.

Uncompressed image files can potentially be huge. This can make adding downloading, uploading or emailing them very difficult and time consuming. Many emails limit the size of the file that can be attached. This means that most uncompressed images, especially high quality ones, cannot be attached to an email without being compressed.

Both the lossy and lossless methods of compression reduce the size of an image by looking for repeating colour patterns within the image. For example, for an image that has a main background colour that is the same throughout the image, a compression method will recognise that there are a lot of pixels that all have the same value and collate them. This means they will be stored as a single data value with further data that records the pattern.

Lossy compression will reduce the file size further by removing detail from the image that should go unnoticed and will not affect the quality too much. One issue with using some lossy compression methods on images, is that the method will remove a little bit of detail each time the image is saved in the compression method e.g. JPEG. This means that there will be a small loss in quality each time it is saved.

1.04 File formats

A file format is the method that we choose to store different data on a computer. Different file formats encode data in different ways. This means that they organise the data for storage in different ways. It is important for software to recognise the file format used to save the data in order to access it.

There are many different types of file format. Some are specific to software and some are more generic or standard. Certain file formats are designed for a particular type of data, for example text, images or multimedia. The file format for a file will mostly depend on the type of data it will be storing. The file format is normally three or four characters, separated from the file name with a dot, and is known as the file extension. These are the most common file extensions:

Table 1.16

File type	File extension	Use
Text	.doc	Microsoft Word document
	.rtf	Rich Text Format file
	.pdf	Portable Document Format
Data	.csv	Comma Separated Values file
	.xls	Microsoft Excel Spreadsheet
	.mbd	Microsoft Access Database
Audio	.mp3	MP3 audio file
	.mid	MIDI file
	.wav	Wave audio file
Video	.mp4	MPEG-4 video file
	.flv	Flash video file
	.wmv	Windows Media Video file
Image	.bmp	Bitmap file
	.gif	Graphical Interchange Format file
	.jpg	JPEG Photo
	.png	Portable Network Graphic

Users often need to import and export data in and out of different software. In order to do this users need the different files to be compatible with each other so that data can be effectively imported and exported. This prompted the development of standard file formats that different software applications can understand.

There are four multimedia standard file formats that you should be aware of:

- Musical Instrument Digital Interface (MIDI) uses a series of protocols and interfaces that allow lots of different types of musical instrument to connect and communicate. MIDI also allows one computer, or instrument, to control other instruments. The controlling device instructs the others on which notes to play and when, whilst specifying the pitch, duration and velocity of each note. MIDI files are, therefore, not a musical recording, but a series of instructions for an instrument to carry out.

- Joint Photographic Experts Group (JPEG) is a standard format for lossy compression of images. It can reduce files down to 5% of their original size.

- MP3 is a standard format for lossy compression of audio files.

- MP4 is a standard format for lossy compression of video files. It can also be used on other data such as audio and images.

MP3 and MP4 have developed from the original file format Motion Picture Experts Group (MPEG). This is a lossy compression method for video files dating back to 1991.

JPEGs, MP3s and MP4s are used in a wide variety of devices, such as computers, digital cameras, DVD/Blu-Ray players and smartphones to store content.

Summary

- As humans we process analogue data but computers process digital data.

- Computers use a binary number system. This consists of a series of 1s and 0s to represent data.

- Computer storage systems are measured in multiples of bytes.

- A register is a small piece of memory where values can be held. Computers use them to hold values for processing.

- Computers do not process hexadecimal notation, they convert it into binary first. Programmers work with hexadecimal notation as it is shorter and easier to read than binary.

- Computers convert text, images and sound into binary to process and store.

- Data compression reduces the size of a file. The two main methods of data compression are lossy and lossless.

- File formats are the method chosen to store data on a computer.

Exam-style Questions

1 A stopwatch uses six digits to display hours, minutes and seconds: (3 marks)

$$0 \quad 1 : 5 \quad 4 : {}_2 \; {}_3$$

It uses a nibble of binary data for each digit displayed on the stopwatch. What time is the stopwatch stopped at when the binary nibbles show the following values?

0000   0010 : 0011   1000 : 0101   1001

2 What is meant by the term 'byte'? (2 marks)

3 The following instruction, written in machine code, is stored in computer memory: (3 marks)

110000011110

Convert the code into hexadecimal notation.

4 Explain why hexadecimal notation is sometimes used to represent binary numbers. (2 marks)

5 Tom wants to send an image by email to his friend Nadia. He needs to reduce the size of the image in order to be able to send it via email. Describe two methods he could use to do this. (4 marks)

6 Tick (✔) the most suitable file extension for the following tasks:

	.jpg	.mp4	.mp3	.csv
Storing holiday photos				
Storing holiday videos				
Storing a favourite song				
Storing data to be imported into other files				

(4 marks)

7 Explain how ASCII is used to represent text so it can be processed by a computer. (2 marks)

8 Kamil and his band want to record the new track they have written. How could the quality of their sound recording on a computer be improved? (2 marks)

20

Chapter 2:
Communication and Internet Technologies

Learning objectives

By the end of this chapter you will:

- understand what is meant by transmitting data and be able to distinguish between serial and parallel transmission, as well as simplex, duplex and half-duplex transmission
- understand and be able to describe different methods of error checking and error detection
- understand the security risks that can arise when using the internet and how they can be minimised
- be able to explain how antivirus and protection software help to protect a user from security risks
- understand the role of the internet browser and internet service provider (ISP)
- understand HTML structure and presentation and what is meant by HTML and hypertext transfer protocol
- understand the concepts of MAC addresses, internet protocol address, uniform resource locator and cookies.

2.01 Data transmission

KEY TERM

Bit – short for binary digit, it is the smallest unit of data in a computer.
Bit rate – the rate at which data is transferred.

The transfer of data occurs either wirelessly by radio waves or over a cable, for example by fibre optic cable or copper twisted wire. The data is transmitted as a stream of **bits**. There are a number of differing methods that can be used to transfer the data.

Figure 2.01 Transfer of data

The rate at which the transfer of data occurs is called the **bit rate**. This is the number of bits that can be transmitted in a given period of time. Bit rate is measured in bits per second (bps) or now more commonly in megabits per second (Mbps). The more megabits per second a data transfer connection is capable of, the quicker the data can be transferred. For example, a broadband connection that has a bit rate of 50Mbps will allow data to be transferred quicker than a broadband connection of 25Mbps.

KEY TERM

Serial transmission – uses a single wire to transfer bits of data.
Parallel transmission – uses multiple wires to transfer bits of data.
Interference – disturbances that can occur in the signals when sending data that may corrupt it.

Serial data transmission

Serial transmission uses a single wire to transfer the data bits. A single wire is cheap to build and can transmit data over long distances. The bits are transmitted sequentially, one bit at a time. There is a set time interval between sending each bit. The time interval depends on the speed of the transmitting and receiving devices. For example, a 56K modem can transmit 57 600 bits per second.

If we consider the 8-bit byte of data 10011001, using serial data transmission the byte would be transferred as shown in Figure 2.02.

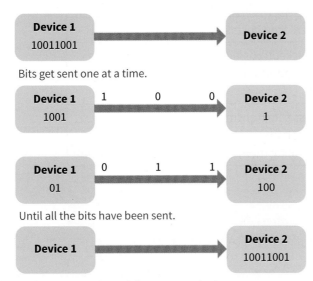

Figure 2.02 8-bit byte of data using serial data transmission

Parallel data transmission

Parallel transmission uses several wires to transfer the data bits simultaneously. For example, with eight wires, 1 byte (8 bits) could be transmitted all at once. Parallel transmission transfers data quicker than serial transmission. However, because there are more cables, parallel transmission is more expensive and is therefore limited to shorter distances.

If we consider the same 8-bit byte of data 10011001, using parallel data transmission it would be transferred as shown in Figure 2.03.

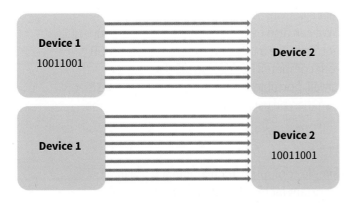

Figure 2.03 8-bit byte of data using parallel data transmission

The byte is sent over multiple wires simultaneously. All bits of the byte are received at the same time.

We can compare the use of serial transmission to parallel transmission:

Table 2.01

Serial transmission	Parallel transmission
Used over long distances	Used over short distances
Uses a single wire	Uses multiple wires
Reduced costs as only single wire needed	Increased costs as multiple wires needed
Slower transmission as data is only transmitted one bit at a time over a single wire	Quicker transmission as data is sent simultaneously over multiple wires
Safer transmission as it is easier to accurately collate the bits together as they are sent one at a time	Less safe transmission as bits are sent simultaneously and errors can occur in collating them together at the receiver's side

SYLLABUS CHECK

Show understanding of the reasons for choosing serial or parallel data transmission.

Identify current uses of serial and parallel data transmission, such as Integrated Circuits (IC) and Universal Serial Bus (USB).

Parallel transmission is quite simple to implement but, because it has multiple wires, **interference** can occur between them. It is because of the level of interference between wires that it is generally limited to short distances of around 5 metres. The same level of interference does not occur with serial transmission as it is only one wire and so the distance of serial transmission can be much further, up to 100 metres.

For many years, parallel transmission was used for data transfer between computers and printers. This is because printers needed data quickly and were generally placed next to computers. Today, parallel transmission has largely been replaced by high-speed serial transmission methods such as the Universal Serial Bus (USB), which transmits data much quicker than parallel transmission. However, this speed comes at a much higher cost and greater level of complexity. We use USB to connect electronic devices to a computer, for example our mobile phones and tablet devices. We can also use it to connect our keyboard and mouse to our computer. To do this we will normally use a USB cable that will have a USB plug. This USB plug will plug into a USB port on our computer. USB is also used in storage devices, for example a USB flash drive. This is a small, portable storage device that has a USB plug to plug the device into the computer. USB can then be used to transfer the data from the computer to the storage device and vice versa.

To learn more about storage devices see Chapter 8.

Parallel transmission is still sometimes used in simple computers such as integrated circuits (IC) where low costs, simplicity and speed are important factors. We often refer to an IC as a microchip. They are used to create microprocessors, which are the small computers that are built into many of the devices we have in our homes, for example a washing machine or a microwave. As ICs are generally built into devices there is little chance for interference to occur and the device can be controlled very quickly through the use of parallel transmission. The internal components of a computer use parallel data transmission to operate.

In order for any data to be sent by serial transmission it needs to be converted. Data is converted from parallel to serial at the sender's side, to be transmitted over a single wire. It is then converted back from serial data to parallel to be processed by the receiver's device. The direction in which the data is transmitted can also vary.

KEY TERM

Simplex transmission – sending data in one direction only at a time.

Duplex transmission – sending data in both direction at the same time.

Half-duplex transmission – sending data in both directions but only one direction at a time.

Simplex transmission

In **simplex transmissions** data is sent in one direction only. Think of it as a one-way street where traffic can only drive in one direction down it. An example is a television broadcast, where data is transmitted to receiving televisions.

Figure 2.04   Simplex transmission

Full duplex transmission

In full **duplex transmissions** data is sent in both directions at the same time. An example is a telephone conversation where both people can speak to each other at the same time.

Figure 2.05   Duplex transmission

Half-duplex transmission

In **half-duplex transmissions** data is sent in both directions but only one direction at a time. An example is a walkie-talkie (two-way radio): both people can speak to each other but only one person can speak at a time. Each person needs to hold down the talk button to speak and then needs to release it to hear the other person speak.

Figure 2.06   Half-duplex transmission

Different methods of data transmission can be combined. For example, a modern network uses serial duplex transmission whereas a walkie-talkie uses serial half-duplex transmission. A mouse uses serial simplex transmission. You can also get parallel simplex, parallel duplex and parallel half-duplex transmissions too.

SYLLABUS CHECK

Identify and describe methods of error detection and correction, such as parity checks, check digit, checksums and Automatic Repeat reQuests (ARQ)

Show understanding of the need to check for errors.

Explain how parity bits are used for error detection.

Error detection and correction

Errors can occur when transmitting and storing data. This is because the channels that are used to transmit the data can be subjected to disturbance. These errors can lead to inaccuracies in the data and make the data unreliable. This is something that we want to avoid, so we use methods of error detection and error correction to increase the accuracy and reliability of the data.

Checksum

A checksum is a simple method of error detection. The number of bits being transmitted is counted up and this numeric count is transmitted with the data. The receiver can then see if the same number of bits has arrived. If the counts match then the receiver knows a full transmission of the data has been received.

Parity check

A parity check uses a parity bit to make sure that that the data has been sent accurately. Data is sent in bytes, normally made up of 8 bits. In a parity check, the first 7 bits of the byte are the data itself, the last bit is the parity bit. A parity check can use odd parity or even parity. All the bits are added together in the byte and depending on whether odd or even parity is being used a 1 or a 0 will be added as the finally parity bit.

If we use the example 1001100, using an even parity check, the parity bit would be a 1:

$$1 + 0 + 0 + 1 + 1 + 0 + 0 = 3$$

As 3 is an odd number we need to add 1 to it to make it even. This is why, when using even parity, the parity bit for this byte will be a 1.

Using the example 1001100 and an odd parity check, the parity bit would be a 0:

$$1 + 0 + 0 + 1 + 1 + 0 + 0 = 3$$

As 3 is an odd number we need to add 0 to it to keep it odd. This is why, when using odd parity, the parity bit for this byte will be a 0.

The devices that the data is being transferred between will be set to check for even parity or odd parity before the data is sent. Parity check is a simple and effective method of error checking. It cannot detect though if disturbance has affected a byte that would still have the same odd or even calculation, but the bits themselves have changed. For example, even parity is being used, the byte 1001100 is being sent with parity bit of 1. If the byte arrived as 110100 with the parity bit of 1, no error would be detected by a parity check as the calculation of the bits is still even. Parity checking is also used on data that is stored as well as data that is transmitted.

Check digits

A check digit is a method of error detection that is used on identification numbers such as barcodes, ISBNs and bank account numbers. It is used to detect human error when entering these numbers. A calculation is performed using the digits in the identification number and a check digit added to the end of the number as a result. The computer will perform the same calculation and compare the result to the check digit. If the two match, it knows the number is correct.

Automatic repeat request

Automatic repeat request (ARQ) is a set of rules for error control when transmitting data. When the device receiving the data detects there is an error with a packet, it automatically sends a request to the device transmitting the data to resend the packet. This resend request will be sent repeatedly until the packet is received error free or a limited amount of resend requests is reached.

TEST YOURSELF

1   Explain the difference between serial and parallel data transmission.
2   Using an example, describe half-duplex data transmission.
3   Explain why parallel transmission is mainly only used over short distances.
4   Explain how a parity check detects errors.

2.02 Security aspects

SYLLABUS CHECK

Show understanding of the security aspects of using the internet and understand what methods are available to help minimise the risks.

There are various security issues that can be encountered when using the internet. The internet itself is a fairly insecure way of transferring data, so security has become a top priority for the everyday user as well as businesses and governments. Security issues can arise for many reasons; it could be when downloading a file, entering data through a web form or sending data via email.

TEST YOURSELF

These are a few of the reasons, can you think of any others?

Good internet security is necessary to protect your personal details, financial details and transactions, as well as downloading and transferring lots of other data. If good internet security is not in place, not only would people's personal computers be attacked, by people such as **hackers**, but it could potentially bring a whole country's economy to a halt if business is affected. This section explains some of the risks you can encounter and how you can avoid them through the use of some good internet security methods.

Figure 2.07 Internet security

SYLLABUS CHECK

Show understanding of the internet risks associated with malware, including viruses, spyware and hacking.

KEY TERM

Hacker – a person who tries to gain unauthorised access to a computer or network.

Malware – a software program that is designed to damage or disrupt a computer.

Virus – a software program that is designed to corrupt a computer and the files on it.

Spyware – a software program that collects user's information through their internet connection.

Hacking – gaining unauthorised access to a computer or network.

Malware

There are risks associated with using the internet that can be harmful to your computer such as **malware**. There are a number of different types of malware that you could encounter, for example viruses and spyware.

Figure 2.08 Internet risks

Viruses

A **virus** is a program that is downloaded on to a computer without the user's knowledge or permission. It is designed to harm a computer and the files that are on it. The most common type of virus will replicate itself over and over until it bring your computer system to a halt. A virus is often spread through sharing files and attachments on emails.

The first known computer virus was called the Creeper virus. It was written by Bob Thomas at a technology company called BBN. The Creeper virus was a test program. It replicated itself and it displayed the message 'I'm the creeper, catch me if you can!' on every system it infected. It was not designed to harm any computers, just to be a demonstration of a computer application. Prior to this, self-replicating programs had not been demonstrated and it was the ability to self-replicate that gained it the name of the first computer virus. A correction program was written called Reaper that deleted the Creeper virus. No damage was left to a computer when the Reaper program was run.

Spyware

Spyware is software that is created to collect information on a user's computer use through their internet connection. The collection of the data is done without the user's knowledge or permission and it is collected normally to be sold on for marketing purposes. It can also gather information such as passwords, bank details and credit card details. These details can then be used to steal the user's identity. Spyware is created by people who want to obtain this data to use it unlawfully. It is often downloaded from untrustworthy websites without the user's knowledge. The spyware hides inside the data downloaded and infects the computer without the user being aware of the action.

As well as collecting information on the user without permission, spyware will also take up some of the bandwidth available for a user's internet connection as it passes back collected information. As a result it can reduce the bandwidth available to the user.

Hacking

As well as the risks above users can also be exposed to **hacking** when using the internet. A hacker is someone who tries to gain unlawful access to a computer or a network by writing a program that will do this. Hackers normally look for a weakness in the setup of a network or computer system and use this as a way to enter. They do this for a number of reasons, such as they may be trying to gain access to money, create a challenge for themselves or it could possibly be out of protest for an issue they want to see highlighted.

A hacker is usually classified as a 'white hat hacker' or a 'black hat hacker'. A white hat hacker exposes security issues in a network or system, but not for unlawful reasons. A white hat hacker can be hired by an organisation to test its own systems to discover any weaknesses that exist. This way those weaknesses can be fixed. White hat hackers are sometimes also known as ethical hackers. A black hat hacker is a hacker that gains access unlawfully.

To learn more about the security issues that can be encountered when using a computer and the internet see Chapter 9.

Protecting against the risks

SYLLABUS CHECK

Explain how anti-virus and other protection software helps to protect the user from security risks.

Firewall – a system that protects unauthorised access to or from a computer or network.

It is possible to protect your computer from attacks that can arise from various issues encountered when using the internet. Anti-virus software can be used to detect a virus attack on a computer system. The anti-virus software will scan the computer's hard disk for any virus attacks and it will remove any that it finds. New viruses are constantly being developed so most anti-virus software will have an update function built into them. This means that when a new virus is discovered, the anti-virus software developers can release an update for computers to detect it

As well as detecting viruses, anti-virus software can be used to detect and remove further malware and spyware. Anti-virus software cannot prevent an attack happening to a computer system, but they can detect it as it is happening and remove the harmful programs. To detect an attack normally a scanning process has to take place. The software scans the computer's hard drive for any viruses. If detected, a virus is removed from the system.

Firewalls are used to monitor transmissions coming into and transmissions going out of a computer or network. Firewalls can be hardware based or software based. Hardware based firewalls are more difficult to compromise but are expensive, whereas software firewalls are cheap, can be easily updated, but can be disabled by a virus.

A firewall uses rules to determine whether an inbound or outbound transmission should be allowed. Some rules, for example those governing email transmission, are determined by the system. Others, such as transmissions for online multiplayer games, can be determined by the user. The firewall allows authorised transmissions to take place, but blocks any transmission that does not conform to the set rules.

Spyware sends outbound transmissions containing stolen data to scammers. Hackers use inbound transmissions to gain access to computers via the internet. Firewalls block these transmissions, thereby protecting the computer.

You can learn more about how to protect against security risks when using the internet in Chapter 9.

1 Describe how a firewall protects a computer or a network.
2 Explain the difference between a virus and spyware.
3 What is hacking?

2.03 Internet principles of operation

Show understanding of the role of the browser and internet server.

KEY TERM

Modem – a hardware device that converts data so that it can be transmitted from computer to computer over telephone wires.

Browser – a program used to access the World Wide Web that displays HTML files.

Packet – a unit of data that can be sent across a network.

Protocol – an agreed format or set of rules to transmit data.

Internet service provider

The internet is a global wide area network (WAN) of interconnected computers and devices. To access the internet we normally need an internet service provider (ISP). An ISP is a company that provides us with access to the internet, normally for a fee. We then use a **modem** to connect our computer to the internet, using the connection provided by the ISP. An older style of connection to the internet that can be used is called a dial-up connection. Dial-up connections use only telephone lines to connect to the internet. They are a cheaper way to connect to the internet, but they are very slow. People or businesses in very remote areas often use dial-up connections as they may not have the cabling in place to use broadband. An alternative way to access the internet is broadband. Broadband connections sometimes uses different cabling to telephone wires, such as fibre-optic cables. They allow a much quicker speed of access to the internet than dial-up connections.

ISPs will have terms of service that a customer will need to adhere to when using the internet. Terms of service are the rules that a customer must follow when using the service from the ISP. They will normally detail any limitations of the service, such as the amount of data a customer can download. It will also cover any legal issues such as using the service for hacking. An ISP will often allow a customer to personalise access to the internet, such as setting a filter that will prevent access to any underage websites.

Internet browser

A website consists of one or more pages of information that can be accessed by other computers on the internet. These pages are known as webpages. A **browser** is a program that allows the computer user to visit, retrieve and display the information that a webpage contains. Content is presented to the user in the form in which it is provided, such as text, images, video and sound. Some forms of content, such as animation, cannot be presented without the use of additional software known as a plugin. Not all plugins work with all browsers.

Figure 2.09 Accessing information across computers on the internet

31

Figure 2.10 Accessing information across computers on the internet

To access a website, the user inputs the website's web address into the browser. This address is known as the site's uniform resource locator (URL). The URL is translated into the unique internet address of the web server that hosts the website. The browser accesses the website determined by the URL and downloads the content. Browsers also allow the user to navigate to different webpages on the website and to other websites via the use of hyperlinks.

Figure 2.11 Web address bar

Web server

A computer that hosts a website is known as a web server. A web server may host many websites. The webserver stores each page of the website and its related content. Retrieving information from a web server is known as downloading. Sending information to a website is known as uploading. A computer that accesses information from a webserver is referred to as a client.

Accessing a website is known as a request. Web servers are designed to handle many requests from many clients simultaneously. Requested information is downloaded from a web server in **packets**. Since each packet consists of only a few bytes, many packets can be sent to many computers in a very short space of time. This means the more bandwidth a web server has access to, the more requests it can handle simultaneously.

As well as hosting websites, web servers are also used to manage facilities such as data storage, online multiplayer gaming and email. Many organisations use web servers on their local area networks to handle email and access to data. Such web servers can only be accessed by a computer on the local area network, making them private.

Although extremely powerful web servers are used to host popular and heavily visited websites, a computer of comparatively limited performance, such as the Raspberry Pi or Arduino, can act as a website host. However, the more limited the web server, the fewer the number of requests it can handle over a given period of time.

> **TIP**
> The Raspberry Pi and Arduino are very small computers that can do most of the tasks performed by a desktop computer. They are not as powerful as a desktop computer, but are great for use in projects such as creating a basic web server.

Even powerful web servers are limited in the number of requests that can be handled, leading to website crashes when too many people try to access the website at once. A good example of this is when tickets are released online for music festivals or sporting events. In these instances the web servers are often unable to handle the number of requests being made.

Furthermore, web servers can be forced offline through what are known as distributed denial of service (DDOS) attacks. With this type of attack, hackers flood the web server with millions of requests. The web server comes to a halt trying to satisfy so many requests simultaneously.

Internet protocols

> **SYLLABUS CHECK**
>
> Show understanding of what is meant by hypertext transfer protocol (http and https) and HTML. Distinguish between HTML structure and presentation.

Hypertext transfer protocol (http) is the core **protocol** that governs transmission of data via the internet. It is an access protocol. Http works as a request–response action. This means that a client (a computer or other device) makes a request that a web server responds to. For example, when visiting a website the client requests, via http, that the information on the website be made available to it. The web server responds by transmitting the website data via http to the client computer.

The actual transfer of the information is governed by another protocol. This is known as the transmission control protocol (TCP). TCP handles the transfer of the data and also checks to ensure the transmission is error free.

Although http is widely used for internet communication, the messages it sends are not particularly secure, making it unsuitable for applications such as banking or internet shopping, where private customer and financial data may be intercepted. Instead, a secure version of http known as https is used. Https encrypts the messages making them extremely difficult to understand by anyone other than the intended recipient that might intercept them.

Figure 2.12 Start of a https address

33

Mark-up language

The transmission a client computer receives from a web server is often in the form of a hypertext mark-up language (HTML) document. An HTML document consists of two parts: the content to be displayed and instructions on how to interpret that content. The language used to convey these instructions consists of mark-ups. Mark-ups are instructions on how content is to be formatted, structured and displayed by the browser. The term originates from the publishing industry where editors would mark-up paper documents from authors with corrections or suggestions. The mark-ups are read and interpreted by the browser, but not displayed.

Mark-ups in HTML take the form of tags. Content that requires formatting in some way is tagged. Tags enclose the content, with an opening tag <> at the beginning of the content and a closing tag </> at the end. Example formatting tags are shown in Table 2.02.

Table 2.02

Opening tag	Tag contents	Closing tag	Output
<b>	emboldens the text	</b>	**emboldens the text**
<h1>	sets the text as a heading in a large font	</h1>	sets the text as a heading in a large font
<a>	defines a hyperlink	</a>	<u>defines a hyperlink</u>
<p>	sets a new paragraph	</p>	sets a new paragraph

Hypertext is text that conveys information and also contains a link to other information, such as another webpage, website, picture, video or sound file. Contained within the hypertext is a hyperlink that is the URL of the additional content. Hyperlinks are named as such because they allow the user to go directly to the linked resource, simply by clicking on the hypertext.

Cascading style sheets

When creating websites, it is usually preferable to separate content and structure from presentation. This is because of the dynamic nature of the internet where many organisations refresh the look and style of their websites on a regular basis to maintain audience interest. However, in many cases the actual content remains the same. By separating the style from the content, the style can easily be changed without having to also change the content and vice versa. Styling mark-up instructions are placed in a separate document known as a cascading style sheet (CSS). Once created, the style sheet can be applied to any HTML document and the document will have its contents presented in the format stated by the style sheet's mark-up instructions.

Figure 2.13 Cascading style sheet (CSS) sample

Cascading style sheets have huge benefits for website designers, as all the pages of a site can be quickly and uniformly updated simply by changing the mark-up instructions in the style sheet. Each HTML page provides the content and structure and the CSS specifies the presentation.

An HTML document is structured into two elements, the header and the body (see Figure 2.14). The header declares the document type (HTML), the page title, and any special instructions for the page, such as plugins to be used or scripts to be run. Additionally, the header includes any CSS that are to be used on the page and where to locate them.

The body contains the content to be displayed, hyperlinks to other pages and if a CSS is not used, any formatting instructions for the content.

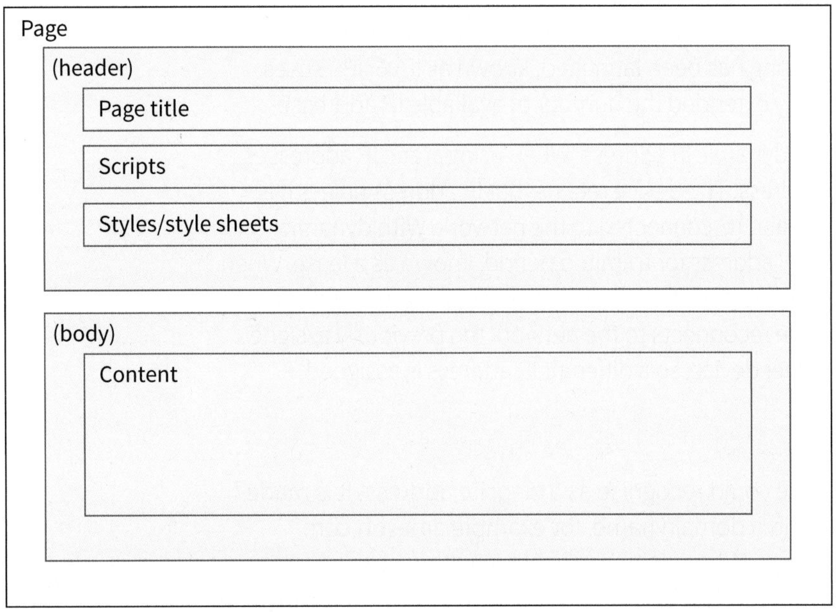

```
Page
  (header)
      Page title
      Scripts
      Styles/style sheets

  (body)
      Content
```

Figure 2.14 HTML document structure

Internet addresses

IP address

Networks and the internet use the transmission control protocol (TCP) for communication. Each device on a network has an address. Just like a house has an address, each device needs an address so that other devices know how to reach it. Without an address other devices would not be able to communicate with the device, as the TCP would not know where to send the communication. The device's network address is known as its internet protocol address (IP address).

Each IP address consists of a 32-bit code. For ease of use, this code is broken down into four groups of three digits, each group being in the range 0 to 255. For example, the IP address of a router on a network could be 192.168.001.255.

In binary, this code would be represented in 32 bits: 11000000101010000000000111111111.

Table 2.03

Denary	Binary
192	11000000
168	10101000
1	00000001
255	11111111

This version of IP addressing is known as IPv4.

Every device connected to the internet has an IP address. As the number of devices connected to the internet has grown, the number of available IP addresses has dramatically decreased. To overcome this a newer version of IP addressing has been launched, known as IPv6. IPv6 uses 128 bits to assign addresses. This has greatly extended the number of available IP addresses.

A device can be assigned either a static or a dynamic IP address. When using static IP addresses, each device is assigned a fixed (static) IP address. The device retains that IP address unless it is changed, even if the device is disconnected and re-connected to the network. With dynamic addresses, the device retains the assigned IP address for a limited period, known as a lease. When the lease period is up, the device is either re-assigned the same address, or assigned another. Additionally, when a device disconnects then reconnects to the network the previously assigned address may have now been taken by another device, so a different IP address is assigned.

Uniform resource locator

A uniform resource locator (URL) is what we could recognise as a website address. It is made up of the access protocol (http or https) and a domain name, for example amazon.com. This URL would be https://www.amazon.com. When visiting a website on the internet, we usually type the website's URL into our browser. The URL is translated by a special type of web server, known as a domain name server, into the 32-bit binary IP address. A URL is far easier for a user to remember than a 32-bit binary number. It also allows an organisation to personalise its web address with the organisation's name.

Figure 2.15 Web address bar

MAC address

Each device on the network also has another address, which is known as its media access control address (MAC address). The MAC address uniquely identifies each device. This address is assigned by the device's manufacturer, unlike an IP address which is assigned by the network. Additionally, the MAC address cannot be changed, unlike a device's IP address. This means a device can be identified, even if its IP address has changed. A MAC address consists of six pairs of two-digit hexadecimal numbers, which are translated into a 48-bit binary code for use by the computer. For example the MAC address 1a2f08a1234c would be 000110100010111100001000101000010010001101001100 in binary (see Table 2.04).

Table 2.04

Hexadecimal	Binary
1a	00011010
2f	00101111
08	00001000
a1	10100001
23	00100011
4c	01001100

Cookies

Cookies are tiny pieces of data that are downloaded by a computer when it visits a website. Cookies are stored by the computer's browser and are accessed by the website whenever it is visited by the client.

Cookies perform various essential tasks. Some are designed to help keep track of whether or not a user has logged in to secure websites, whilst others store dynamic data such as the items the user has added to an online store's shopping basket. Without cookies these facilities would not be available. However some cookies are used for purposes that can raise concern. Some websites use cookies to track a user's internet surfing activities and then tailor online adverts to match the user's interests. Others are used to store sensitive information such as passwords and credit card details, which can then be accessed at a later date. Cookies can be declined by the user or removed from the computer if the user has concerns. Both actions can usually be performed by the device's browser.

Summary

- Data can be transmitted in different ways, along a single wire as serial transmission or multiple wires as parallel transmission. Data can also be transmitted in different directions, in one direction at a time as simplex transmission, both directions at a time as duplex transmission, or in both directions but only one direction at a time as half-duplex transmission.
- Errors can occur when transmitting data so there are methods for error detection and correction, such as parity checks, check digit, checksums and Automatic Repeat reQuests (ARQ)
- Security risks such as malware, including viruses, spyware and hacking can arise when using the internet. These risks can be minimised through the use of software and hardware such as anti-virus software and firewalls.
- An ISP is a company that provides a connection to use the internet, normally for a fee.
- A browser is a program that allows a user to visit, retrieve and display the information that a webpage contains. A computer that hosts a website is called a web server. https is a more secure version of http used for banks, shopping and other sites that need added security in transmitting personal information.
- HTML is the language that webpages are written in. An HTML document consists of two parts, the content to be displayed and instructions on how to interpret that content. The instructions on how to display the content is done through the use tags known as mark-ups.
- Each computer or device has a unique address called a MAC address. This is an address that is fixed to that device and cannot be changed. When using the internet, each computer or device is assigned an IP address, which can be static or dynamic.
- We use a URL to access a website. It is normally typed into the address bar of a computer and is made up of the access protocol and the website domain name.
- Cookies are tiny pieces of data that are downloaded by a computer when it visits a website. Cookies are stored by the computer's browser and are accessed by the website whenever it is visited by the client.

Exam-style questions

1 Explain what is meant by bit rate. (3 marks)

2 Describe two advantages of serial data transmission. (2 marks)

3 Draw a line to match the error detection and correction terms to the correct definitions: (4 marks)

Check digit	The number of bits transmitted are added up and this calculation is transmitted with the data
Parity check	A 1 or a 0 is added as an extra bit to make the sum of the bits in a byte odd or even
Checksum	A digit added when transmitting data from a calculation performed on the digits in the data
Automatic repeat request	A request that is sent by the receiving device to tell a sender that there is an error in the data being received

4 Explain how anti-virus software protects a computer. (2 marks)

5 Sami wants to access a website that sells his favourite records. Explain how Sami will do this. (2 marks)

6 The Rock Factory uses a CSS to store the formatting instructions for their website. Explain what the advantages are for doing this. (2 marks)

7 Describe the difference between a static IP and a dynamic IP. (4 marks)

8 Why can the use of cookies raise concern for an internet user? (6 marks)

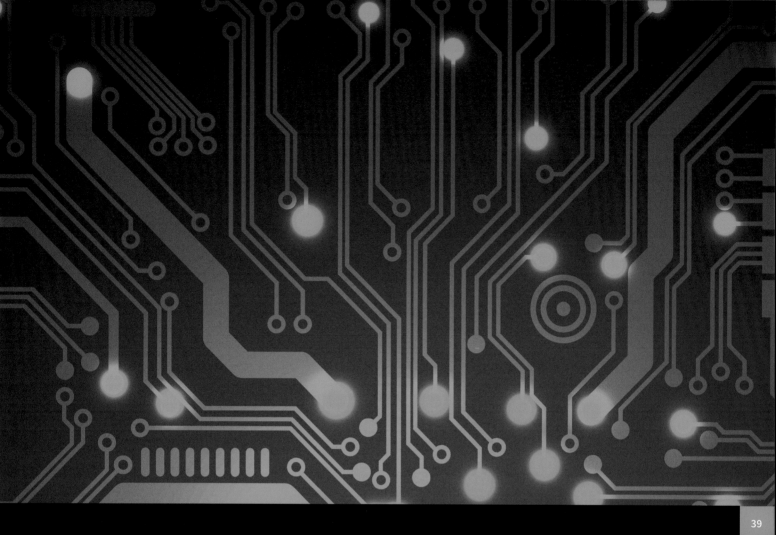

Chapter 3:
Computer Architecture, Languages and Operating Systems

Learning objectives

By the end of this chapter you will:

- understand the basic von Neumann architecture for a computer system
- be able to describe the fetch–execute cycle
- be able to describe the purpose of an operating system
- understand the need for interrupts
- understand what high-level and low-level languages are and why both are needed
- understand the need for compilers, interpreters and assemblers.

3.01 Von Neumann architecture

SYLLABUS CHECK

Show understanding of the basic Von Neumann model for a computer system and the stored program concept (program instructions and data are stored in main memory and instructions are fetched and executed one after another).

In 1945 John von Neumann, a Hungarian mathematician, physicist and inventor, proposed a model to create a computer system. Prior to the von Neumann model computers were usually built to carry out one kind of task. If they were needed to carry out a different task they would need to be completely rebuilt. For example, Alan Turing's Electronic Numeric Integrator and Computer (ENIAC) machine could perform complex calculations, but in order to perform a different set of calculations it would take around three weeks to rewire it. The idea that led to the development of the von Neumann model was to create a machine that would be much easier to re-program.

Figure 3.01 The ENIAC Machine

The von Neumann architecture model proposed that not only should the data being processed be stored in memory, but that the instructions being used to process the data should also be stored in the same memory. This would make it much easier to reprogram the system as a different set of instructions could be used to process the data more easily.

The von Neumann architecture, on a simple level, states that a computer system can be thought to consist of three main sections:

- The central processing unit (CPU) – the main processing unit of the system, also known as the processor.

- Storage – Primary memory (also known as main memory) is fast to access and is directly accessible by the processor. RAM and ROM form main memory, along with **cache memory** and **registers**. Secondary storage (also known as backing storage) is slow to access and is not directly accessible by the processor. Instead, communication with secondary memory is through input/output controllers. Hard drives and CD-ROMs are examples of secondary memory.

- Input and output devices – are used to communicate with other devices, for example, a keyboard (input) or printer (output).

To learn more about RAM and ROM, see Chapter 8.

KEY TERM

Cache memory – a portion of memory used for high-speed storage.

Register – an internal memory location within the CPU that temporarily holds data and instructions during processing.

Accumulator – the register that is used for arithmetic and logic calculations.

These three sections can be further separated into several main components:

- **Control Unit (CU)** – This is an internal part of the CPU and it controls the flow of data through the CPU. It also controls the interactions between the different parts of the CPU. It tells the different components, as well as any linked hardware, how to respond to the instructions given.

- **Immediate access store (IAS)** – This is the memory found inside a CPU and is used to hold not only data but also the instructions needed to process that data. It is also more commonly known as the CPU memory. The CPU needs to hold the data and instructions here before processing as it would be much too slow bringing them directly from the main memory to be processed. The data and instructions are firstly loaded into the main memory and then brought into the IAS to be processed.

- **Arithmetic Logic Unit (ALU)** – This is an internal part of the CPU that carries out calculations on data. The arithmetic part uses the usual operators such as multiply, divide, add and subtract. The logic part carries out comparisons such as 'equal to', 'greater than' and 'less than'. Values need to be placed in the **accumulator** for calculations to be carried out.

- **Registers** – These are internal memory locations within the CPU. They temporarily hold data and instructions during processing. Registers are used to move data and instructions into and around the different components of the CPU.

- **Input/Output** – These allow interaction with the computer. Instructions are processed from and to them in the CPU.

- **Buses** – The components of the model need to be connected to one another and this is usually done through buses. A bus is a series of conductors, or pathways, which can be considered a sort of 'highway' for information. Three separate buses are used:

  ○ The data bus carries the data.

  ○ The address bus carries the memory address.

  ○ The control bus carries the instructions.

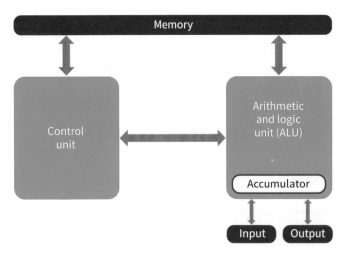

Figure 3.02 The von Neumann architecture

In von Neumann architecture, instructions and data are both stored as binary numbers.

You can learn more about data and instructions stored as binary numbers in Chapter 1.

The stored-program concept

The von Neumann architecture is based on the concept of a stored-program computer. A stored-program computer is a computer that stores programs and instructions in digital memory. This concept is thought to be older than the von Neumann architecture itself and is what inspired its development. A modern stored-program computer is one that keeps its programmed instructions, as well as its data, in read–write, random-access memory (RAM). Before a computer can actually read data, process it and produce information, it must read a set of instructions called a 'program'. The program will state what processing is required. In many computer systems it is possible for more than one program to be stored in the computer at any given time. The only requirement is that sufficient storage locations are available for both the program and the necessary data. This is termed 'multiprogramming'.

The fetch–execute cycle

Describe the stages of the fetch–execute cycle, including the use of registers.

Von Neumann created an architecture with a single processor that follows a linear sequence. This sequence is called the 'fetch–execute cycle':

Step 1 – Fetching the instruction

The CPU fetches the necessary data and instructions and stores them in its own internal memory locations (the IAS).

To fetch the instruction the CPU uses the address bus. The CPU puts the address of the next item that needs to be fetched on to the address bus. Data from this address is then moved from main memory into the IAS in the CPU by travelling along the data bus.

Registers are then used to store and move the data to a special register that will decode the instruction.

Step 2 – Decoding the instruction

The CPU now needs to understand the instruction it has just fetched. To do this it needs to decode the instruction.

Every CPU is designed to understand a specific set of commands. This is called the 'instruction set' and the CPU uses this in order to decode the instruction.

The moving of data and the decoding of instructions is controlled by the CU.

Step 3 – Executing the instruction

Now the CPU understands the instruction, it can execute the instruction.

This is where any processing of the data that is needed for the instruction takes place. The CPU basically carries out the instruction. If any arithmetic calculations are needed in the instruction this will be carried out by the ALU.

Once the CPU has executed the instruction the cycle can begin again for the next instruction.

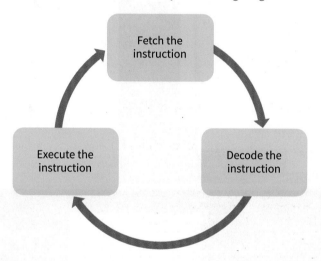

Figure 3.03 The fetch–execute cycle

TEST YOURSELF

1   Describe the function of the arithmetic and logic unit.
2   Explain the stored-program concept.
3   Describe the purpose of buses in the von Neumann architecture.

3.02 Operating Systems

SYLLABUS CHECK

Describe the purpose of an operating system.

Every computer or device needs an operating system (OS) to run other programs. Therefore an operating system is a vital piece of software for a computer. An OS is the framework that allows us to communicate with computer hardware in an interactive way. Without this, we would not be able to tell the computer to do anything and it would not have any instructions to follow.

Operating systems perform basic tasks, such as recognising input from the keyboard, sending output to the display screen, keeping track of files and controlling peripheral devices such as printers.

Microsoft Windows is an OS that is available for personal computers and is now also available on some tablet and mobile technologies. Two other examples of OS are MAC OS X and Linux.

A modern OS uses a graphical user interface (GUI) to allow the user to interact with the computer. This kind of interface is made up of icons, buttons and menus that can be clicked to carry out tasks. The layout of these features can differ from company to company with each aiming to create the perfect user layout.

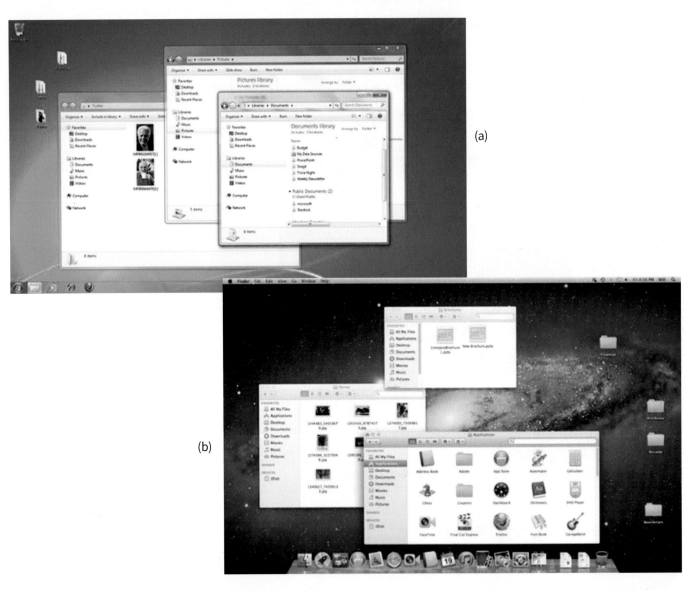

Figure 3.04 (a) Windows 7 GUI (b) MAC OS GUI

Before operating systems developed to have a GUI, they had a command line interface (CLI). In this type of interface a user would need to type in the different commands they would like to carry out on the operating system. Some users still use a CLI operating system; an example of this is Linux.

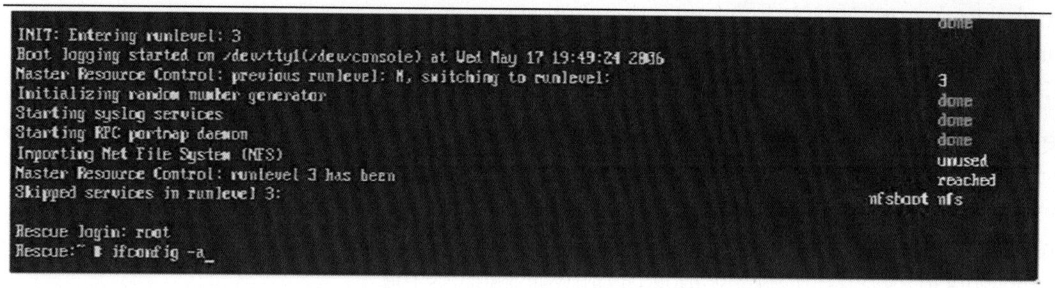

```
INIT: Entering runlevel: 3                                              done
Boot logging started on /dev/tty1(/dev/console) at Wed May 17 19:49:24 2006
Master Resource Control: previous runlevel: N, switching to runlevel:    3
Initializing random number generator                                    done
Starting syslog services                                                done
Starting RPC portmap daemon                                             done
Importing Net File System (NFS)                                         unused
Master Resource Control: runlevel 3 has been                            reached
Skipped services in runlevel 3:                               nfsboot nfs

Rescue login: root
Rescue:~ # ifconfig -a_
```

Figure 3.05 CLI operating system Linux

An OS has several main functions:

- It provides the GUI for the user to interact with the computer.

- It manages the hardware and **peripherals** that are connected to the computer.

- It manages the transfer of programs into and out of memory. The OS will manage how the programs will be placed into the available memory.

- It divides the processing time between the different applications that are running. This allows a user to have multiple applications running at a time, such as playing music on the computer whilst completing work in word processing software, as well as finding information on the internet.

- It manages security for the computer, such as anti-virus software and firewalls, and manages access rights (the amount of information a user is allowed access to).

- It manages file handing, allowing users to store, delete and move files on a computer. It keeps track of all actions carried out on files.

- It manages utility software on the computer such as disk defragmentation and disk formatting software.

KEY TERM

Peripheral – a hardware device, used to input, store or output data from a computer, that is not directly part of the computer itself.

Without an operating system a computer would basically be rendered useless as it wouldn't be able to load any software and we would not be able to interact with it.

3.03 Interrupts

SYLLABUS CHECK

Show understanding of the need for interrupts.

An interrupt is a signal. When this signal is received it will inform software that something has happened, an event has occurred. An interrupt could be generated by many sources. It could be generated by a user pressing keys on a keyboard, it could be from a printer connected to the computer. The signal will come from a device attached to the computer or from a program within the computer.

An interrupt will cause the operating system on a computer to stop and then the operating system will need to work out what to do next. After an interrupt is detected, the operating system will either continue running the program it was currently running or it will begin running a new program.

A computer can only run one program at a time, but because the program it is currently running can be interrupted to run another program, it can perform multiple tasks. It will take it in turns to run the programs so that it appears to be running them at the same time. This is called 'multitasking'. It is the ability to do this that means that we can listen to music on our computer, whilst completing work in a word processing application, whilst surfing the internet for information.

An OS will contain a program called an interrupt handler. The role of the interrupt handler is to prioritise the interrupt signals as it receives them and places them in a queue to be handled.

There are two main categories of interrupts, hardware interrupts and software interrupts. These denote where the interrupt has come from. An example of a hardware interrupt is one that is generated when a peripheral such as a keyboard or a printer produces the signal. An example of a software interrupt is when an application is opened or closed on a system.

TEST YOURSELF

1 Describe the role of an interrupt.
2 Explain why a computer would be useless without an operating system.

3.04 High-level and low-level languages

SYLLABUS CHECK

Show understanding of the need for both high-level and low-level languages.

High-level languages are designed to be used by humans as they are much closer to what humans recognise in terms of language. This means that high-level languages are much easier to read and write programs in than either **low-level languages** or **machine code**.

All computers only process machine code. This is written in binary as a series of 1s and 0s. As humans, we would find it very difficult and time consuming if we had to program using machine code, so programming languages were developed. To learn more about binary numbers, see Chapter 1.

High-level languages

The first high-level languages were developed in the 1950s. One of the very first was FORTRAN (short for 'formula translation'). This was invented in 1954 by John Backus for IBM to be used as a practical alternative to **assembly language** in programming scientific and engineering projects. FORTRAN was released for sale to the public in 1957. FORTRAN is now more than 60 years old and it is still widely considered an excellent language by scientific programmers. The development of further high level languages followed; the most common include BASIC, C, C++, C#, Pascal, Java and Python.

Figure 3.06 John Backus, creator of FORTRAN.

The reason behind the development of high level languages is that they are closer to the language and **syntax** that we as humans understand. This advantages of this are that high-level languages are much easier for humans to read. Also fewer mistakes are made when programming in a high-level language as not as much knowledge is needed for the languages that control the workings of a computer, such as machine code and assembly language.

The features of a high-level language are that it deals with structures such as variables, arrays, loops, conditions, functions and procedures, whereas machine code deals with memory addresses, registers and operation codes. To learn more about variables, arrays, loops, conditions, functions and procedures, see Chapter 11.

KEY TERM

High-level language – a programming language that looks like the language humans generally use.

Low-level language – a programming language that is closer to the native language of computers.

Machine code – a series of binary numbers, made up of 1s and 0s.

Assembly language – a low-level programming language that uses mnemonic codes to create programs.

Syntax – the structure of language in a computer program.

Compiler – a computer program that takes a whole program written in a high-level language and translates it into machine code.

Interpreter – a computer program that translates a program written in a high-level language line by line into machine code.

Source code – code in its text-based form that is yet to be translated into machine code.

Executable file – a file format that a computer can directly process.

Programmers can create programs and software in a high-level language. This can then be translated into machine code for a computer to process. As well as the advantage of high-level languages being easier to read and write, they are also mostly independent of any hardware they are run on, unlike assembly language which is specific to the hardware it runs on. Therefore a computer programmer can write programs in a high-level language and they can be run on any kind of computer. In high-level languages, one line of code could do several different tasks.

The following code is an example of a program in Python:

```
name = input ("What is your name?")
print ("Hello " + name)
```

In the first line of code above, the program is creating a variable called 'name'. It is creating a place for the user to input some data. It outputs a question 'What is your name?' for the user. In the variable 'name' it has created, it will store the data that the user inputs. So in one line of code it is doing at least four things.

In the second line of code it is creating an output that will display the text 'Hello'. It is then recalling the data that is stored in the variable 'name' and displaying that also. Therefore in two lines of code this small program is doing at least seven things.

In order to be read by a computer, high-level languages need to be translated into machine code. This translation is done by a **compiler** or an **interpreter**.

A compiler

Show understanding of the need for compilers when translating programs written in a high-level language.

A compiler is a computer program that takes code written in a high-level language and translates it into machine code. The code produced by a programmer is called **source code**. This source code is written generally written in a high-level language and needs to be translated into machine code to be read by the computer. A computer can only process machine code, so unless a high-level language is translated a computer will not understand it.

The act of running the source code through the compiler is called compiling the code. As compiling the code is essential to a computer understanding it, each high-level language has its own compiler.

As a compiler translates the whole of the source code in one go, if there are any errors in the code it will not compile. The compiling process will stop and these errors will need to be removed before the program can be compiled. The machine code from the compiler is output as an **executable file** (.exe). This file will contain the whole of the machine code needed for the CPU to process the program that has been written. The file can then be stored for future use whenever the program is needed.

Error handling is an important feature of a compiler. Most programmers will not write a perfect program on their first attempt. The compiler will run through the program and produce a report of all the errors it detects. A programmer can then use this report to go back to their source code and fix the errors to make their program error free, so that it will compile and run.

An interpreter

An interpreter is also a computer program that takes code written in a high-level language and translates it into machine code. Unlike a compiler, which takes the whole of the source code and translates it in one go, an interpreter translates the source code into machine code one line at a time.

If there are any errors in the program they will be detected when that line of source code is reached. This is a great advantage of an interpreter; each line of code can be checked as a programmer is writing it, as each line of code is translated in turn. With a compiler, the programmer would need to wait for the whole of the program to be compiled before they can read the error report.

As an interpreter translates each line of code in turn, it takes up less memory than a compiler, which needs to generate an executable file to be stored.

As each line of code is translated immediately, on the surface it seems as if an interpreter would be quicker when translating code. However, as an interpreter has to analyse and translate each line of code to run the program each time, they are mostly slower than compilers, which may initially take time to compile the code, but will then run it much quicker once compiled.

Low-level languages

The raw code that a computer processes is called machine code. In its most raw form this would be a series of binary numbers. Machine code can also be referred to as 'object code'. Machine code is very difficult to understand but it can be represented in a slightly simpler fashion as assembly language.

Assembly language assigns **mnemonic codes** to sets of machine code to make them more understandable. Some examples of mnemonics are:

- **ADD** – this would be an instruction to use addition in a calculation

- **SUB** – this would be an instruction to use subtraction in a calculation

- **INP** – this would be an instruction that would require a user to give an input

- **OUT** – this would be an instructions that would output data

Low-level languages are basically a computer's native language. Assembly language and machine code are both examples of a low-level languages. Machine code is directly executable by a computer and assembly language uses software called an **assembler** to be converted into machine code. An assembler is a computer program that will take the basic instructions (mnemonics) used in assembly language and convert them into machine code so they can be processed by the computer. Assembly language was the first progression from machine code to make writing programs simpler. High-level languages then developed at a later stage.

In low-level languages each line of code will perform only one task. The following code is an example of a simple addition program in assembly language with a command and its explanation on the right (after #):

```
INP          #asks the user to give an input e.g. a number
STA ONE      #stores the number input in an address named ONE
INP          #asks the user to give a 2nd input e.g. a number
ADD ONE      #adds the second input to the number stored in ONE
OUT          #outputs the result
HLT          #stops the program
ONE DAT      #assigns the name ONE to the next data location
```

We can see that each line of code performs only one task.

Low-level languages are still used to program certain software. Software applications, such as device **drivers** for hardware, for example a graphics card, need to communicate effectively with the computer they are connected to. This means that when you buy a piece of hardware such as a graphics card or printer you will need to download the correct drivers that enable it to communicate with the computer in which it has been installed. Without the driver, the two cannot communicate. Driver software is written in a low-level language. Low-level languages are mostly still used where very close control of the processing in the CPU is needed.

KEY TERM

Mnemonic codes – instruction codes used in assembly language.

Assembler – converts assembly language into machine code.

Driver – a program that controls a device, for example, a printer or a keyboard.

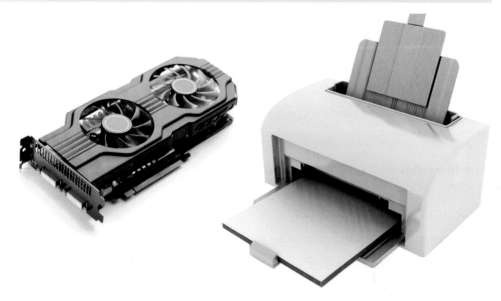

Figure 3.07 A graphics card and a printer need drivers to communicate with a computer; drivers are still mainly written in low-level languages

Table 3.01 compares low-level with high-level languages.

Table 3.01

Low-level language	High-level language
Examples include machine code and assembly language	Examples include C, Java and Python
Difficult for humans to understand but can be easily executed by a computer; a computer's native language	Much easier for humans to understand and much closer to natural language
Needs an assembler to be processed	Needs to be translated by a compiler or an interpreter
One line of code does one thing	One line of code can do several things

Summary

- The von Neumann architecture was designed to be easier to re-program.

- The von Neumann architecture is based on the concept of a stored-program computer, which keeps its programmed instructions as well as its data in read–write, random-access memory (RAM). Before a computer can read data, process it and produce information, it must read a set of instructions called a 'program'. The program will state what processing is required.

- The von Neumann architecture has a single processor that follows a linear sequence, the fetch–execute cycle. The CPU will fetch an instruction from the main memory to its internal memory before decoding and executing the instruction. It does this through the use of registers and buses.

- Every computer or device needs an operating system to run other programs. Operating systems perform basic tasks, such as recognising input from the keyboard, sending output to the display screen, keeping track of files and controlling peripheral devices such as printers.

- An interrupt is a signal that informs software that an event has occurred.

- High-level languages are designed to be used by humans as they are much closer to what humans recognise in terms of language. They need to be run through a compiler or an interpreter to be processed by a computer.

- Low-level languages are basically a computer's native language. Low-level languages can be processed by a computer without being run through a compiler or an interpreter.

- A compiler is a computer program that takes the whole of a program written in a high-level language and translates it into machine code.

- An interpreter is a computer program that translates a program into machine code line by line.

- Assembly language assigns mnemonic codes to sets of machine code to make them more understandable. An assembler converts assembly language back into machine code.

Exam-style questions

1   Describe the fetch–execute cycle carried out in the von Neumann architecture.   (3 marks)

2   Define the term 'register'.   (2 marks)

3   Draw a line from each term to its correct definition: (4 marks)

Control unit		Connection between components in the CPU along which information travels
Arithmetic and logic unit		Unit that manages the flow of data through the CPU
Accumulator		Register in which values are stored to have calculations carried out on them
Bus		Unit that carries out calculations on data in the CPU

4   Describe three functions of an operating system.   (3 marks)

5   Describe two advantages of high-level languages.   (2 marks)

6   Explain the difference between a compiler and an interpreter.   (2 marks)

7   Describe the role of an assembler.   (1 mark)

8   Tick (✔) which statements are true and false about low-level languages: (4 marks)

Statement	True	False
Low-level languages are a computer's native language		
Low-level languages need to be compiled before they can be processed		
Low-level languages are much easier for humans to understand		
In a low-level language one line of code will perform one task only		

Chapter 4:
Logic Gates

Learning objectives

By the end of this chapter you will:

- understand and be able to define the functions of AND, OR, NOT, NAND, NOR and XOR logic gates
- understand the binary output produced by the logic gates when two inputs are given (only one input will be given in a NOT gate)
- be able to produce a truth table from a logic gate
- be able to determine a logic gate from a truth table
- be able to produce a logic circuit to solve a given problem
- be able to produce a logic circuit for a given logic statement.

4.01 Types of logic gate

A **logic gate** is a basic foundation of a **digital circuit**. Data and instructions are both stored and transmitted by digital computers as the binary digits 0 and 1. (To learn more about binary digits see Chapter 1.)

Various tasks are performed in a computer by switching on a high **voltage** or a low voltage through a digital circuit called a logic gate. High voltage is represented by the binary digit 1 and low voltage is represented by the binary digit 0. Some circuits may only have a few logic gates, others, such as a **microprocessor**, could have thousands. Each logic gate controls the flow of electronic signals in a predetermined way.

Each logic gate that we will look at, except a NOT logic gate, will have two inputs and one output. A NOT logic gate will only have one input and one output. We can work out what the output of a logic gate will be from different inputs, using the rules of each different logic gate.

KEY TERM

Logic gate – the basic foundation of a digital circuit that controls the flow of electronic signals.

Digital circuit – a circuit where electronic signals are one of two values, high voltage (1) or low voltage (0).

Voltage – the potential difference across an electrical component needed to make electricity flow through it.

Microprocessor – an integrated circuit that provides the same functions of a CPU.

Truth table – a way of showing every outcome of a logic gate.

SYLLABUS CHECK

Understand and define the functions of NOT, AND, OR, NAND, NOR and XOR (EOR) gates, including the binary output produced from all the possible binary inputs (all gates, except the NOT gate, will have 2 inputs only).

Recognise and use standard symbols to represent logic gates: NOT, AND, OR, NAND, NOR and XOR.

The AND gate

When using an AND logic gate the output (X) will only be high voltage if both inputs (A and B) are high voltage. This means that X can only be 1 if A and B are 1.

We can write logic statements to represent a logic gate or logic circuit. Logic statements are also known as 'Boolean statements' or 'Boolean logic'. A logic statement for an AND gate is:

$$X = A \text{ AND } B \quad \text{or} \quad X = A.B$$

A dot (.) can be used to represent the word AND in a logic statement.

The AND logic gate is represented by the symbol shown in Figure 4.01.

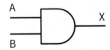

Figure 4.01 AND logic gate symbol

This logic gate has the labels A and B for the inputs and X as the output. The logic of this circuit is that if A AND B are 1 then X will be 1. If either A or B are 0 then X will be 0.

Truth tables

SYLLABUS CHECK

Draw truth tables and recognise a logic gate from its truth table.

A **truth table** is a way of showing every outcome of a logic gate. The value of each input is shown along with the value that will be output as a result of these inputs. We can represent the logic of the AND gate in a truth table as shown in Figure 4.02.

Input		Output
A	B	X
0	0	0
0	1	0
1	0	0
1	1	1

Reading a truth table

If A = 0 and B = 0 then X = 0

If A = 0 and B = 1 then X = 0

If A = 1 and B = 0 then X = 0

If A = 1 and B = 1 then X = 1

Figure 4.02 Logic of the AND gate in a truth table

With two inputs to the AND gate, there are four combinations and two possible outcomes.

The OR gate

When using an OR logic gate the output X will be high voltage if input A or input B is high voltage. This means that X will be 1 if A or B is 1.

As a logic statement we could write this as:

$$X = A \text{ OR } B \qquad \text{or} \qquad X = A+B$$

A cross sign (+) can be used to represent the word OR in a logic statement.

The logic gate OR is represented by the symbol shown in Figure 4.03.

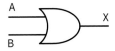

Figure 4.03 OR logic gate symbol

The logic of this circuit is that if A or B are 1 then X will be 1. If A and B are 0 then X will be 0.

We can represent the logic of this gate in a truth table.

Table 4.01

Input		Output
A	B	X
0	0	0
0	1	1
1	0	1
1	1	1

With two inputs to the OR gate, there are four possible outcomes.

The NOT gate

When using a NOT logic gate there is only one input and one output. The output X will be high voltage only if the input is low voltage. This means that X will only be 1 if A is 0.

As a logic statement we could write this as:

$$X = \text{NOT A} \qquad \text{or} \qquad X = \bar{A}$$

A line, called a vinculum, over an input label can be used to represent the word NOT in a logic statement.

The logic gate NOT is represented by the symbol shown in Figure 4.04.

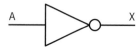

Figure 4.04 NOT logic gate symbol

We can represent the logic of the NOT gate in a truth table:

Table 4.02

Input	Output
A	X
0	1
1	0

With one input to the NOT gate, there are two possible outcomes. In a NOT gate, the output is always the opposite of the input.

As well as producing a truth table for a logic gate it is important that we can recognise a logic gate from a truth table. To do this we need to look at the output of the logic circuit and at the inputs that go into it. We need to recall the rules of each logic gate and see which set of rules are being applied to the inputs to achieve each output. For example, if we can see that the output is only 1 when both inputs are 1, from the rules we know this is an AND gate.

Logic gates can be combined. When certain types of logic gates are combined they create another type of logic gate.

The NAND gate

The NAND logic gate is a combination of an AND gate followed by a NOT gate. The output X will be high voltage unless both inputs are high voltage. If both inputs are high voltage the output will be low voltage. This means that X will always be 1 unless A and B are 1.

As a logic statement we could write this as:

$$X = \text{NOT (A AND B)} \qquad \text{or} \qquad X = \overline{A.B}$$

The logic gate NAND is represented by the symbol shown in Figure 4.05.

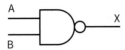

Figure 4.05 NAND logic gate symbol

Broken down into the two original logic gates before they are combined, it would be as shown in Figure 4.06.

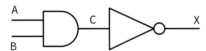

Figure 4.06 Logic gates NOT and NAND before they are combined

We can represent the logic of the NAND gate in a truth table. To understand this logic gate more easily we will refer to the interim output/input in Table 4.3 as C, as shown in Figure 4.06:

Table 4.03

Input		Interim	Output
A	B	C	X
0	0	0	1
1	0	0	1
0	1	0	1
1	1	1	0

We would complete a truth table like this by setting each of the starting inputs to either 1 or 0, writing down what that will give as an interim value, then taking that interim value and writing down what that would give as a final output.

For example, the first line of the truth table states that both inputs A and B are 0. We know that if either input A or B in an AND gate are 0, then the output will always be 0. Therefore, we write down 0 as the interim value.

We then use this interim value as the input for the next logic gate. We know that if the input to a NOT gate is 0, the output will always be the opposite, so 1. Therefore we write down 1 as the output for X. With two inputs to the NAND gate there are four possible outcomes.

We need to make sure that for the input values we have covered every combination of 0 and 1 that could occur. As we can see with the AND gate above, we could have 0 and 0, 1 and 0, 0 and 1, 1 and 1 as combinations.

The NOR gate

The NOR logic gate is a combination of an OR gate followed by a NOT gate. The output X will be high voltage unless both inputs are high voltage. If either input is high voltage the output will be low voltage. This means that X will always be 0 unless A and B are 0.

As a logic statement we could write this as:

$$X = NOT \ (A \ OR \ B) \quad \text{or} \quad X = \overline{A+B}$$

The logic gate NOR is represented by the symbol shown in Figure 4.07.

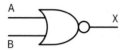

Figure 4.07   NOR logic gate symbol

Broken down into the two original logic gates before they are combined, it would be as shown in Figure 4.08.

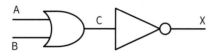

Figure 4.08   Logic gates NOT and OR before they are combined

To understand this logic gate more easily we will refer to the interim output/input as C in the truth table:

Table 4.04

Input		Interim	Output
A	B	C	X
0	0	0	1
1	0	1	0
0	1	1	0
1	1	1	0

With two inputs to the NOR gate, there are four possible outcomes.

The XOR (EOR) gate

An XOR or Exclusive OR gate has a slightly changed logic from an OR gate. Similar to an OR gate, the output X will be high voltage if either of the inputs are high voltage. However in an XOR gate, if both inputs are high voltage, the output will be low voltage. This means that X will always be 1 if inputs A and B are different.

As a logic statement we could write this as:

$$X = (NOT \ A \ AND \ B) + (A \ AND \ NOT \ B) \quad \text{or} \quad X = A \oplus B$$

58

The logic gate XOR is represented by the symbol shown in Figure 4.09.

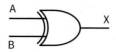

Figure 4.09 XOR logic gate symbol

We can represent the logic of the XOR gate in a truth table:

Table 4.05

Input		Output
A	B	X
0	0	0
0	1	1
1	0	1
1	1	0

With two inputs to the XOR gate, there are four possible outcomes.

When we start to combine a series of logic gates, working out the output value can be very challenging.

4.02 Logic circuits

SYLLABUS CHECK

Use logic gates to create electronic circuits.
Produce truth tables for given logic circuits.

A logic circuit is an electronic circuit that combines a number of logic gates. The gates in the logic circuit will control the flow of electricity through the circuit.

Creating a truth table for a logic circuit

A logic circuit using an AND, an OR and an XOR logic gate is shown in Figure 4.10.

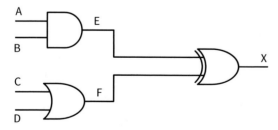

Figure 4.10 Logic circuit using an AND, OR and XOR logic gate

We have added interim values to this logic circuit to help us work out the output. In the truth table we will refer to these as work space as they are needed to work out the output. A truth table for this would look like Table 4.06.

59

Table 4.06

Input				Work space		Output
A	B	C	D	E	F	X
0	0	0	0	0	0	0
1	0	0	0	0	0	0
0	1	0	0	0	0	0
1	1	0	0	1	0	1
0	0	1	0	0	1	1
1	0	1	0	0	1	1
0	1	1	0	0	1	1
1	1	1	0	1	1	0
0	0	0	1	0	1	1
1	0	0	1	0	1	1
0	1	0	1	0	1	1
1	1	0	1	1	1	0
0	0	1	1	0	1	1
1	0	1	1	0	1	1
0	1	1	1	0	1	1
1	1	1	1	1	1	0

We would complete this truth table by starting at the top left of the circuit. It is often a good place to start by setting all the input values in the first gates to 0. Therefore, we would write down that input A and B are both 0.

We know that if either input into an AND gate is 0, the output will be 0. Therefore, we would write down the output from this gate, which we have labelled as E, is 0.

We would then look at the logic gate below the AND gate, which is an OR gate. We again can start by setting both input values to 0. We know that if both input values are 0 in an OR gate, the output will be 0. Therefore we would write down the output from this gate, which we have labelled as F, as 0.

We then move to the next logic gate that outputs E and F go to, which is an XOR gate. E and F now become the inputs for this gate. We know that if both inputs for an XOR gate are 0, the output will be 0. Therefore we can write down that output X is 0.

As there are more inputs into this logic circuit, there are more combinations that can occur. We need to make sure that we have covered all combination that could occur across the four initial inputs, for example 0000, 1000, 0100, etc. When we have four inputs into a logic circuit it creates 16 possible combinations.

Figure 4.11 shows a logic circuit using a NAND, a NOR and an OR gate:

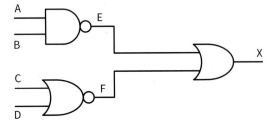

Figure 4.11 Logic circuit using a NAND, NOR and OR gate

We again have added extra labels to this logic circuit to help us work out the output. In the truth table we will refer to these as work space. A truth table for this would look like Table 4.07:

Table 4.07

Input			Work space			Output
A	B	C	A	B	C	A
0	0	0	0	1	1	1
1	0	0	0	1	1	1
0	1	0	0	1	1	1
1	1	0	0	0	1	1
0	0	1	0	1	0	1
1	0	1	0	1	0	1
0	1	1	0	1	0	1
1	1	1	0	0	0	0
0	0	0	1	1	0	1
1	0	0	1	1	0	1
0	1	0	1	1	0	1
1	1	0	1	0	0	0
0	0	1	1	1	0	1
1	0	1	1	1	0	1
0	1	1	1	1	0	1
1	1	1	1	0	0	0

Creating a circuit diagram from a logic statement

SYLLABUS CHECK

Produce a logic circuit to solve a given problem or to implement a given written logic statement.

A logic circuit can also be written in the form of a logic statement. From this logic statement we can produce a logic circuit diagram.

Let us look at the following logic statement:

$$X = NOT(A \ OR \ B)$$

From looking at this statement we can see that we will need to use the logic gates NOT and OR. We can see the output X will come from a NOT gate.

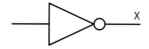

Figure 4.12 NOT logic gate

The interim input into this NOT gate comes from the output of an OR gate. This OR gate has two inputs, A and B. Figure 4.13 shows the logic circuit for the statement X = NOT(A OR B).

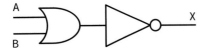

Figure 4.13 Logic circuit for the statement X = NOT (A OR B)

Let us look at another logic statement:

$$X = (NOT\ C)\ AND\ (A\ OR\ B)$$

From looking at this statement we can see that we will need to use the logic gates AND, NOT and OR. We can see the output X will be determined by NOT C and A OR B. Therefore, it is the AND gate that output X will come from. The AND gate will link the NOT and the OR gates.

We have noted that the output X will come from an AND gate:

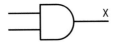

Figure 4.14 AND gate

Into the AND gate will be a NOT logic gate with an input of C:

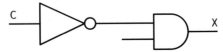

Figure 4.15 NOT logic gate with an input of C into the AND gate

Also into the AND gate will be an OR gate with the inputs A and B:

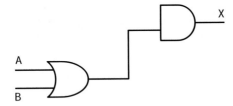

Figure 4.16 OR gate with inputs A and B into the AND gate

Figure 4.17 shows the full logic circuit for the logic statement X = (NOT C) AND (A OR B).

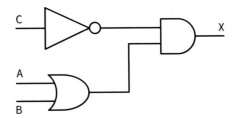

Figure 4.17 Full logic circuit for the statement X = (NOT C) AND (A OR B)

TEST YOURSELF

Produce a truth table for the logic circuit in Figure 4.17?

Creating a logic circuit to solve a problem

We can also create a logic circuit to solve a problem.

In a system there are three buttons (A, B and C) and a lamp (X). The lamp only comes on if B or C are pressed, but not if they are pressed together. If A is pressed the lamp goes off even if B or C are pressed.

If we start to think about the logic of this problem we can see that if NOT(A is pressed) AND (B is pressed or C is pressed, but not together) then X will light up.

Therefore, as a logic statement this would be X = (NOT A) AND (B XOR C).

Now we have a logic statement for our problem we can create our logic circuit. We can see from our logic statement that the output will need to come from an AND gate. Going into this AND gate will need to be a NOT gate with an input of A and an XOR gate with inputs B and C.

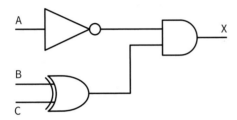

Figure 4.18 Full logic circuit using AND, NOT and XOR gates

TEST YOURSELF

Produce a truth table for the logic circuit in Figure 4.18?

Summary

- Various tasks are performed in a computer by switching on a high voltage or a low voltage through a digital circuit called a logic gate. Each logic gate controls the flow of electronic signals in a predetermined way.

- When using an AND logic gate the output (X) will only be high voltage if both inputs (A and B) are high voltage.

- When using an OR logic gate the output X will be high voltage if input A or input B is high voltage.

- When using a NOT logic gate there is only one input and one output. The output X will be high voltage only if the input is low voltage.

- The NAND logic gate is a combination of an AND gate followed by a NOT gate. The output X will be high voltage unless both inputs are high voltage. If both inputs are high voltage the output will be low voltage.

- The NOR logic gate is a combination of an OR gate followed by a NOT gate. The output X will be high voltage unless both inputs are high voltage. If either input is high voltage the output will be low voltage.

63

- An XOR or Exclusive OR logic gate has a slightly changed logic from an OR gate. Similar to an OR gate, the output X will be high voltage if either of the inputs are high voltage. However, in an XOR gate, if both inputs are high voltage, the output will be low voltage.

- A truth table is a way of showing every outcome of a logic gate.

- A logic circuit is an electronic circuit that combines a number of logic gates. The gates in the logic circuit will control the flow of electricity through the circuit.

Exam-style questions

1   Describe the role of a logic gate in a logic circuit. (1 mark)

2   Consider the following logic circuit:

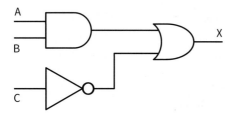

   a Write the logic statement to represent this logic gate. (3 marks)

   b When A = 0, B = 0 and C = 1, output X = ... (1 mark)

   c When A = 1, B = 0 and C = 1, output X = ... (1 mark)

3   Draw the logic circuit for the logic statement X = (A OR B) AND C. (2 marks)

4   The following truth table is for the logic statement X = A XOR (B AND C) (3 marks)

Fill in the missing values to complete the truth table.

Input			Output
A	B	C	X
0	0	0	
1	0	0	1
0		0	0
1	1		
	0	1	0
1	0	1	1
0	1		1
1	1	1	

5   In a system there are three switches and an alarm. The alarm will sound only if switches A and B are on. If switch C is turned on then the alarm will stop.

   a Write the logic statement for this problem. (2 marks)

   b Draw the logic circuit for this problem. (2 marks)

   c Create a truth table for this problem. (2 marks)

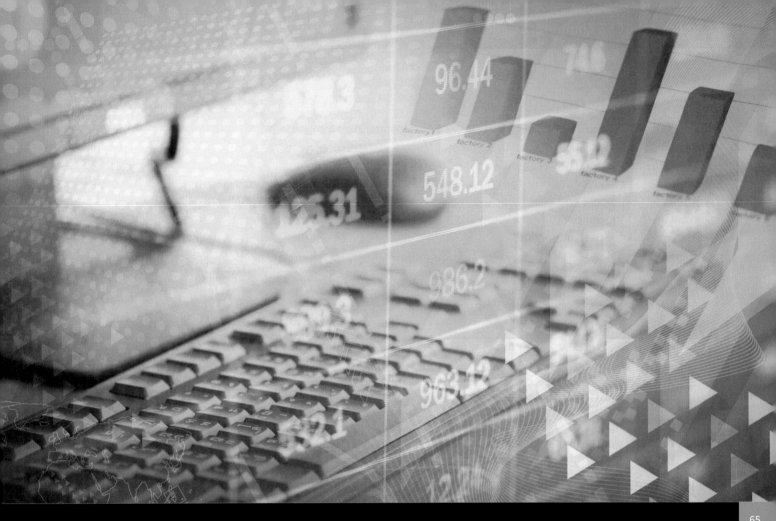

Chapter 5:
Input Devices

Learning objectives

By the end of this chapter you will:

- be able to define the term 'input device'
- be able to describe how a keyboard and a mouse are used
- be able to describe how 2D and 3D scanners work, including barcode readers and quick response (QR) code readers
- be able to describe how digital cameras capture and store images
- be able to describe how touch screens and interactive whiteboards are used
- be able to describe how microphones record sound and how they are used
- be able to describe how input devices are used in real-life scenarios.

5.01 What is an input device?

An input device is a **hardware** device that allows a user to enter data into a computer system. Input devices can be manual or automatic. Manual input devices need a user to physically enter the data into a computer system. For example, a keyboard requires a user to press the keys to enter data into the computer. An automatic input device is one that will automatically read data and input it into a computer system. For example, a temperature sensor can take the temperature of a room and automatically input it into a computer system without any user interaction.

KEY TERM

Hardware – the physical components of a computer.

There are a number of input devices that we need to be aware of and we need to be able to explain how each of them works.

TEST YOURSELF

Why would we want computers to read data automatically into a computer system for us?

SYLLABUS CHECK

Describe the principles of operation (how each device works) of a range of input devices including 2D and 3D scanners, barcode readers, digital cameras, keyboards, mice, touch screens, microphones.

Describe how these principles are applied to real-life scenarios, for example: scanning of passports at airports, barcode readers at supermarket checkouts, and touch screens on mobile devices.

5.02 Keyboard

Keyboards are one of the main and most common methods of entering data into a computer. They have a set of keys that can be pressed to enter the data. The keys will generally allow entry of letters, numbers and symbols that are used in our everyday language. They can also

Figure 5.01 A keyboard is a hardware device used to input data into a computer system

have special command and function keys that are programmed to perform specific tasks, as well as arrow keys that can be used to navigate the computer system.

More modern devices can have an on-screen keyboard. This is similar to a normal keyboard, but the keys are not keys that are physically pressed down. They are keys that are displayed on a screen and when pressure is applied to a 'key' they will enter the data of that key. They are created by **software** rather than being a hardware device. On-screen keyboards can also be known as virtual keyboards.

KEY TERM

Software – programs and instructions run on a computer.

Figure 5.02 An on-screen keyboard is a software device used to input data into a computer system

Table 5.01

Advantages of a keyboard	Disadvantages of a keyboard
Keyboards are very simple to use	It is easy to make a mistake when using a keyboard to input data
If a person is trained to type fast then inputting data using a keyboard can be very efficient	If a person is not trained to type fast then inputting data using a keyboard can be slow

TEST YOURSELF

Can you think of three different devices that would make use of an on-screen keyboard?

There is a further type of keyboard available to input data, which is called a 'concept keyboard'. A concept keyboard is generally a surface that is flat and has a grid of buttons on it. Each button in a concept keyboard can be programmed do a specific task. An overlay can then be placed over the buttons to indicate the tasks that they perform.

A concept keyboard can be used where there is a limited amount of data that needs to be entered into a system, for example in a fast food restaurant. Each item of the menu could be assigned to a different button, with a button to total the order when complete. This way each order can be input quickly, increasing the speed at which orders can be taken.

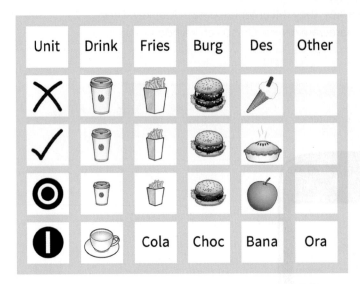

Figure 5.03 An example of what a concept keyboard may look like

5.03 Mouse

A mouse is an input device that is used to control a pointer or a cursor on a screen. It enables a user to move the pointer to navigate around the screen. The user can then use the buttons that are generally part of a mouse to click items on the screen. A mouse will normally have two buttons at the top. The left button will often allow a user to click on an item and the right button, when clicked, will normally open up a menu. A mouse could also have a scroll wheel in the centre of the two buttons that can be used to scroll through documents and webpages.

An older style of mouse will probably have a ball in the underside of it. This rolls against internal rollers in the mouse to move the pointer in the direction intended. A newer style of mouse uses an optical laser that tracks the movement of the mouse across a surface to move the pointer in the direction intended.

Figure 5.04 This older style of mouse uses a roller ball to move the pointer

Figure 5.05 This newer style of mouse uses an optical laser to move the pointer

Table 5.02

Advantages of a mouse	Disadvantages of a mouse
A mouse is very simple to use	The user needs a flat surface next to the computer to move the mouse around in. If this space is limited it can restrict the use of a mouse
A mouse lets the user efficiently navigate around a screen	If the roller ball gets clogged with dirt, or if dirt covers the optical laser, this can stop a mouse working properly

There are two alternative pointing devices: a trackball and a foot mouse. A trackball is used in the same way as a mouse but it is useful where desk space is limited. The user rotates the ball whilst the main body part stays still. It has buttons like a standard mouse. The trackball mouse allows users to move and select items on the screen and is often used in computer-aided design (CAD) especially for 3D design, for its increased precision compared to a mouse. Trackballs have also been adapted for those users who have limited hand movement in the form of a foot mouse.

TEST YOURSELF

CAD is a type of software that is used to create precise drawings. CAD can be used to create 2D drawings and 3D models and it is used by people such as architects and engineers.

Figure 5.06 A trackball   Figure 5.07 A foot mouse

5.04 Scanners

2D scanner

Two-dimensional (2D) scanners can be used to scan a physical document, for example a printed image or a text document, from a flat (two-dimensional) surface. 2D scanners can be used to convert these documents into a digital format that can be used on a computer.

A scanner works by shining light into the surface of the document. The light source moves across the document and the reflected light is captured onto a light-sensitive device using mirrors and lenses. The captured image is converted into a digital signal for input to a computer.

Most documents that are scanned will be stored as an image. However, a scanned document can be manipulated and stored in different formats. Text can be converted to a text file using **optical character recognition (OCR)** software, so that it can be edited. However, this is not very reliable and can be prone to errors; a converted document is often full of mistakes.

A 2D scanner can also be used with **optical mark recognition (OMR).** With OMR, the scanner scans a page and the OMR software notes where marks have been made on it. The computer records the marks' positions as inputs. This method is widely used to automatically mark multiple-choice question papers. It is also used in situations where it is preferable to avoid the user having to handwrite text, for example recording the numbers on a lottery ticket.

KEY TERM

Optical character recognition (OCR) – a process where text on a scanned document is recognised and converted to digital text.
Optical mark recognition (OMR) – a process where scanned marks on a page are automatically converted to inputs.

There are two main types of 2D scanner: a flatbed scanner and a handheld scanner.

Figure 5.08 A flatbed scanner scans a document automatically

A flatbed scanner is the most popular type of 2D scanner. With a flatbed scanner an image is placed on the scanner bed, this is the base of the scanner. The scanner moves the light and sensor itself and scans the whole image automatically. This is the type of scanner that you may have used at school.

A handheld scanner is an alternative type of scanner. With a handheld scanner the light and sensor must be manually pushed along the image to scan it. Handheld scanners are normally used to scan smaller images.

Figure 5.09 A document must be manually scanned with a handheld scanner

TEST YOURSELF

Think of two examples where a handheld scanner would be more suitable than a flatbed scanner?

Table 5.03

Advantages of a scanner	Disadvantages of a scanner
Flatbed scanners are able to produce digital copies of documents that are quite high in quality	Scanned documents can use a lot of memory space, especially if they are scanned photographs
Digital copies created by a 2D scanner can be edited with software such as graphics creators, photograph editors and word processors	Although the scanned digital copy can be quite high in quality, it is not likely to be as high quality as the original, especially if it is an image or photograph
A digital copy of a scanned document could be attached to an email or included in another digital document	If the quality of the original document is not very good then the quality of the scanned image is likely to be even worse

3D scanner

A three-dimensional (3D) scanner is used to produce a 3D model rather than a 2D image. A 3D scanner will scan a 3D object using a laser or a light source (or sometimes X-rays). It will measure and input the geometry of an object into a computer system and create a model of it. This model could be a digital model or, if used in conjunction with a 3D printer, a physical model or replica.

3D scanners are now used as a security measure in airports. An airport traveller will step into the 3D scanner, their body will be scanned and a 3D image of their form will be displayed for inspection to see if they are carrying any hidden goods or weapons on their body.

Figure 5.10 A 3D scanner in an airport used as a security check

Biometric devices also make use of scanners. They are used to identify people. A person's biological features are scanned, for example their retina, their fingerprint or their face, and the data from these is stored in a computer system. When a person's biological features are scanned again, a biometric device will look for a match in the computer system.

KEY TERM

Biometric device – device that recognises human physical characteristics, such as fingerprints.

In many airports today biometric data can be used to allow users to enter into a country. The biometric data is stored a chip in a person's passport. This passport can then be scanned to input the person's biometric data. The person will step into a biometric scanner that will scan their biometric features to see if they match those stored in the chip in the passport.

The biometric data used in this situation is generally facial recognition software. The facial recognition software will take in a lot of measurements about a person's face. For example the distance between a person's eyes and the length of a person's nose will be stored on the chip in the passport. A facial scanner in an airport will use facial recognition software to see if the measurements of the face it is scanning match the measurements stored on the passport chip. This kind of passport is referred to as an electronic passport, or e-passport for short.

To learn more about different types of biometric devices see Chapter 9.

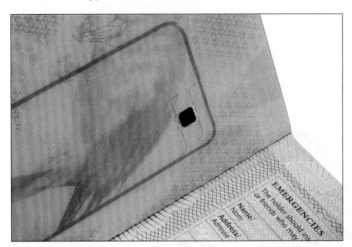

Figure 5.11 An e-passport

Barcodes

Barcodes were developed in the 1970s to help people in the retail trade. Cashiers were starting to get health problems, such as repetitive strain injury (RSI), from entering all the prices of a customer's shopping basket for hours on end. A method needed to be developed that would allow the price of a shopping item to be input into the cash register without continuous typing by the cashier. This led to the development of the barcode and barcode scanner.

Barcodes are represented by black vertical bars with spaces (white vertical bars) between them. A barcode reader is an input device with software that converts data that is pre-coded into a barcode. The barcode reader scans the barcode and translates it into a number. Barcodes are printed on every product sold and bought. Since the data is scanned and read automatically, barcode readers provide a fast and reliable method of entering data.

When a barcode is scanned, it is illuminated with a red light called an illuminator. A **sensor** inside the reading device detects the light reflected back from the barcode. The signal received is an **analogue** signal. The sensor converts the analogue signal into a **digital** signal. The digital signal is then decoded by a decoder. Once decoded the signal is sent to a computer. This could also be our mobile phone.

 KEY TERM

Sensor – a device that records physical inputs.
Analogue – a signal, or data, that constantly varies.
Digital – a signal, or data that consists of two states, 1 or 0.

In a supermarket, the barcode data read is matched with the product's information, such as the product name, code and manufacturer. The price of the product is not stored in the barcode; it is stored in the computer system and is matched up to the product details when the product is scanned. This is so that if the price of a product changes, all the barcodes don't need to be changed on a product, the price can just be changed in the computer system. Data such as the price of a product will be stored in a database.

To learn more about databases see Chapter 14.

The barcode data is used to form the customer's bill and also to assist in stock checks. Once a product is sold, the stock figure a store has recorded for that product can be automatically reduced by one, so that a fairly accurate amount of that product in stock can be recorded. This stock figure may not be completely accurate as it will not account for any stock that is stolen from the shop. Barcode readers can either be flatbed or handheld scanners.

Figure 5.12 A barcode being scanned

Figure 5.13 A handheld barcode scanner

Table 5.04

Advantages of a barcode	Disadvantages of a barcode
A barcode is a very efficient method of entering a product's details to find out its price	If the barcode is damaged, not printed clearly, or rubbed away in part, it may not scan properly
A barcode can be used to help keep a record of stock levels for a product	If the barcode data has not been recorded in the computer system, the barcode scanner will not be able to find it

QR codes

A quick response (QR) code is a 2D square barcode. They look like Figure 5.14:

Figure 5.14 Quick response (QR) code

While there are a few claims to the origin of the QR code, it is most commonly believed to have been invented by Denso-Wave (part of the Toyota group) in 1994 to track parts when manufacturing vehicles.

QR codes are made up of lots of black and white squares. Each black or white square is called a module. You will notice that the example QR code in Figure 5.14 has three larger squares in three of its corners. These squares tell a QR code reader where the edges of the QR code are.

A normal barcode is one-dimensional; it stores data in a line of black and white bars. QR codes are two-dimensional; they store data both horizontally and vertically. The means that they can also be read horizontally and vertically by a QR code reader. A barcode can normally store up to 30 numbers, while a QR code can normally store about 7000. It is their ability to store this amount of data that makes QR codes useful for creating links and storing things.

To read a QR code we need a QR code reader. This can be a simple imaging device such as the camera on a smartphone. The imaging device coupled with QR code reading software will allow us to create a QR code reader. When we scan the QR code with a QR code reader it will show what was encoded into it. This could mean we are directed to a website that will open or a message could be displayed. QR codes can be coded so they link to many things, for example, a website, a video or a social networking profile. They can also be used to store data such as a message or a telephone number. Using a QR code reader, try reading the QR code in Figure 5.14.

Anyone can make a QR code. There are lots of websites we can use to make them such as www.qrstuff.com and www.qr-code-generator.com. These website are QR code generators. We can enter the data we want to be encoded into a QR code and the generator will create a QR code for us.

QR codes are very clever as they have an error correction method built into them, called the 'Reed Solomon method'. This means that even if the QR code has a couple of misprinted modules or a couple of modules are covered up, the QR code can normally still be read.

TEST YOURSELF

Find out more about how the Reed Solomon method works as an error correction method.

People and companies use QR codes for a large variety of reasons. They are an excellent marketing tool. They can be placed in an advert allowing the audience to scan the code leading them to more product information. QR codes are used on business cards to link a person to further information about a business, such as their website, or a person's full resume. They can also be used in museums or on wildlife and nature trails to provide the audience with further information should they want it.

Table 5.05

Advantages of a QR code	Disadvantages of a QR code
QR codes are a very efficient method of storing information and linking to it	QR codes are not yet as common as barcodes. There may be some people that do not know what they are for
QR codes can store a variety of information including links to websites, images, videos and messages	If QR codes are used for advertising or for distributing information, people need to have the ability to read them, such as using a smartphone
Even if some areas of a QR code are missing or covered up, the code can often still be read	

5.05 Digital camera

Steven Sasson, an engineer at Kodak, invented and built the first known digital camera in 1975. A digital camera **encodes** digital images and videos and stores them for viewing and later use. Prior to this cameras were analogue devices and would use camera film to capture images. This film would need to be processed in a dark room to be able to view the images taken with the camera.

 KEY TERM

Encoding – the process of converting data or information to a particular form.

With a digital camera images can be viewed immediately. The image is stored in built-in memory or on an SD card and can be displayed on a screen. Most cameras sold since the early 2000s have been digital cameras. Many mobile phones now have a digital camera built into them.

Digital cameras capture an image by recording the image via a sensor called a charge-coupled device (CCD). The recorded image is then stored on the memory available to the camera and can be viewed on a screen. This file can be uploaded to a computer to be stored for the future. It can also be shared via email or social networking sites to show to friends and family.

The larger the number of pixels the CCD is capable of, the higher the quality of the image that can be taken. The quality of a digital camera is measured in pixels. If an image was zoomed in enough we would be able to see lots of very little squares of colour. These are the 'picture elements' (called 'pixels') and they are what an image is made of. In a poor-quality image it is quite easy to see these pixels when the image is enlarged. A camera on a mobile phone is normally about 3 or 4 megapixels (1 megapixel is 1 million pixels) whereas a professional camera could be 28 megapixels.

Table 5.06

Advantages of digital cameras	Disadvantages of digital cameras
An image taken with a digital camera can be immediately seen on a screen. Therefore the user can decide if they want to take another image instantly if they think that one is not good enough	If a digital camera only has a very small number of pixels, the quality of the image it can take may be lower than that of a camera that uses film
A backup copy can be made of any digital images taken. If the original copy of the images is then lost, the user still has a copy of them in the backup	When an image is taken with a digital camera you can immediately see it. It can also be immediately shared. Sharing the image could be accidental if they user didn't mean to do so. A user may accidental share images that they did not want to share
Images taken with a digital camera can easily be shared as they are an electronic copy. They can easily be attached to emails or uploaded to social networking sites	If a user has a lot of digital images taken with a digital camera they may require additional storage space. This could mean they need a larger SD card for the camera
An image taken with a digital camera can be easily edited as it is an electronic file	

5.06 Touch screen

A touch screen is an interactive device that combines a liquid crystal display (LCD) with touch-sensitive sensors. The sensors recognise simple touches, either by finger or by a stylus. The screen determines which part of the screen has been touched and, according to the application utilising it, translates the input into an action, such as simulating the clicking of an 'OK' button or selecting a drop-down menu. Additionally users can input text by touching keys on a virtual keyboard.

More complex touch screens can recognise gestures such as swipes or pivots. These gestures allow more complicated interactions, for example:

- switching between applications

- rotating an image

- increasing or decreasing the zoom on a document which is too large to fit on the screen

- drawing a picture by finger or stylus.

Touch screens are normally capacitive or resistive. A capacitive touch screen uses the natural electrical signals that we have in our bodies to detect when we are touching the screen. A touch screen that is capacitive will not be able to detect these signals through a glove. This is why when we have gloves on and try to use some touch-screen phones, the screen does not detect our touch. A resistive touch screen has multiple layers with space in between. When slight pressure is applied to the screen the layers touch and the device recognises that we are touching the screen.

Figure 5.15 Mobile phones often feature an interactive touch screen for input and output

Touch screens are considered to be a user-friendly device as the user can interact directly with whatever application or data is displayed. They are ideal for use with small devices such as smartphones, tablets, e-readers, PDAs and car satellite navigation systems because they eliminate the need for separate input and output devices. In fact without touch screen technology, such devices could not exist in their current form and would be much larger and more cumbersome to use. Touch screens are also used on much larger devices where a keyboard and mouse input system would be unsuitable, such as kiosk interactive tables in museums and exhibitions.

Due to their nature, touch screens can be quite imprecise. A finger touches the screen over a large area, making it very difficult to pinpoint a particular spot on the screen. Many touch screen interfaces use icons and large virtual buttons to overcome this issue. Alternatively some touch screens allow the use of a pen, or stylus, for precise control.

Figure 5.16 Tablets feature an interactive touch screen for input and output

Table 5.07

Advantages of a touch screen	Disadvantages of a touch screen
Touch screens are very simple to use	Touch screens can be quite imprecise, making it difficult to touch the required position accurately
Touch screens save space as they combine a screen and an input device in one	Inputs might not be possible if the screen is damaged

5.07 Interactive whiteboard

An interactive whiteboard acts as a virtual whiteboard. It works in a similar manner to a touch screen, except that the board is an input device only. It connects to a computer via a universal serial bus (USB) interface. (To learn more about USB, see Chapter 2.)

The computer's visual display is projected onto the board. The board is then calibrated (adjusted) to make sure the sensors it contains line up with the displayed image. The user touches the board either with a special pen or their finger. Sensors determine which part of the board has been touched and translates the touch into an action, for example selecting a menu option or clicking an 'OK' button. The input acts like a mouse pointer.

Interactive whiteboards come with their own special software that means they can be used like a real whiteboard, for example we can handwrite on it or draw diagrams. The software also allows actions to be carried out such as moving of objects around the screen. Additionally, the software allows:

- handwriting recognition: The user can handwrite text onto the board that is translated into digital text.

- PC control: Applications can be run and controlled via the board's input.

- text input: A virtual keyboard can be displayed on the whiteboard and text input this way can be entered directly into a document or web browser.

Interactive whiteboards can be used in many different situations such as:

- education, at schools, colleges and universities: Their ease of use means that they are suitable for users of all ages and capabilities.

- sport: Interactive whiteboards are used in team planning and strategy sessions to help put across and discuss tactics.

- business: Interactive whiteboards are often used in meetings for discussion and for staff training.

Figure 5.17 Interactive whiteboards can be used in education

Figure 5.18 Interactive whiteboards can be used in business

Table 5.08

Advantages of an interactive whiteboard	Disadvantages of an interactive whiteboard
Interactive whiteboards are quite versatile – they be can written on, drawn on, display images and text	Interactive whiteboards must be accurately calibrated before use otherwise a user may touch the board in one place and the touch isn't registered
Interactive whiteboards offer a large screen that is excellent for use in a classroom or business environment	Interactive whiteboards can be quite imprecise, which can make it difficult to do any work that requires more complex detail

5.08 Microphone

A microphone is an analogue input device that records sound. Since computers operate digitally, the analogue sound wave must be converted into digital format before the computer can process it. The operation is performed using an **analogue-to-digital convertor (ADC)**. To learn more about analogue and digital data see Chapter 1.

 KEY TERM

Analogue-to-digital convertor (ADC) – a device that converts analogue data into digital data.

Once in a digital format, the computer can save the sound in a file for later use. It can also transmit it to another computer. An example of this would be video conferencing, where a microphone is used to record and transmit speech from one user to another over the internet.

Additionally, the input from a microphone can be used for voice recognition:

- Speech-to-text software allows the user to speak words which the computer records and converts to text in a document. This system is ideal for users who have difficulty typing or for disabled users who have limited or no use of their hands.

- In-game speech allows video game players to communicate with each other when playing over the internet. The microphone is usually built into the player's headset.

- Speech input is now becoming used to control video game consoles and smart televisions. The speech instructs the console or television what application to run or what channel to switch to.

Figure 5.19 A microphone records analogue sound

Figure 5.20 Speech recognition systems are becoming more popular in the home such as in an Xbox 360 Kinect

One disadvantage of using microphones for speech recognition is that the sound might not be recorded clearly or be understood correctly. Users have individual speech patterns and accents, not all of which are easy to understand for a computer. This can lead to incorrect input or no action occurring as the computer will not know what to do. To overcome this issue, speech recognition software allows users to train the computer to recognise their speech.

Table 5.09

Advantages of using a microphone	Disadvantages using a microphone
Microphones allow the use of speech recognition systems	Sound might not be accurately recorded
Disabled users with hand and finger impairment can use a microphone to input commands to a computer	Speech recognition systems have to be trained before they can be used properly

Summary

- An input device is a hardware device that allows data to be input into a computer system.

- Keyboards are one of the main and most common methods of entering data into a computer. A concept keyboard is a specialist keyboard with limited, specialised functions.

- A mouse is an input device that is used to navigate to a point on a screen. There are different types of mouse such as a trackball and a foot mouse

- 2D scanners scan a physical document by shining light into the surface of the document.

- 3D scanners produce a 3D model, rather than a 2D image, using a laser or a light source (or sometimes X-rays).

- Biometric devices use scanners to identify people.

- Barcodes are codes represented by black and white vertical bars. A barcode reader scans a barcode and translates it into a series of numbers.

- QR codes are made up of black and white squares. QR codes can link to many things such as a website, a video or a social networking profile. QR codes are scanned and read using a QR code reader.

- A digital camera records and encodes digital images and videos and stores them.

- A touch screen is an interactive device that combines an LCD visual display with touch-sensitive sensors. The sensors recognise simple touches.

- An interactive whiteboard is a virtual whiteboard that works in a similar manner to a touch screen. Interactive whiteboards are widely used in education, business and sport.

- A microphone is an analogue input device that records sound.

83

Exam-style questions

1   Identify two input devices that could be present in a mobile phone.   (2 marks)

2   Explain what is meant by an input device.   (1 mark)

3   Input devices can be either automatic or manual. Explain the difference   (2 marks)
    between the two types. Give examples in your answer.

4   Explain how a business could make use of QR codes.   (2 marks)

5   Explain how a touch screen device recognises that the screen is being touched. (4 marks)

6   Explain why, when using a microphone, an analogue-to-digital converter is   (3 marks)
    also needed when inputting data.

7   Describe two benefits of using a digital camera over a film camera.   (4 marks)

8   Describe how an interactive whiteboard could be used to help train staff in   (2 marks)
    a company.

9   Describe how a barcode works and what data they usually store.   (4 marks)

10 Explain how a 3D scanner works. Give an example in your answer.   (3 marks)

Chapter 6:
Sensors

Learning objectives

By the end of this chapter you will:

■ be able to define the term sensor

■ understand how a range of sensors input data into a computer system

■ describe how a range of sensors are used in many areas of our lives.

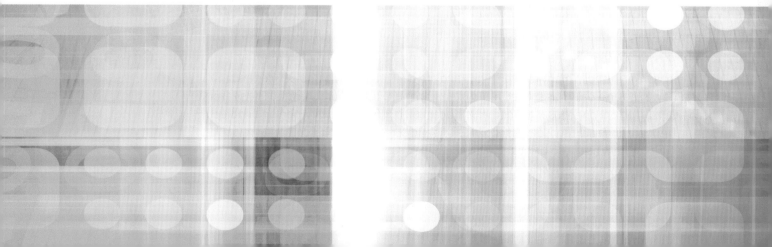

6.01 Introduction

SYLLABUS CHECK

Describe how a range of sensors can be used to input data into a computer system, including light, temperature, magnetic field, gas, pressure, moisture, humidity, pH and motion.

Describe how these sensors are used in real-life scenarios, for example: street lights, security devices, pollution control, games, and household and industrial applications.

A **sensor** is another type of input device. It is a device that records data about the physical environment around it. This data is output in the form of a signal for a computer to process. It is this signal that becomes the input of data for the computer.

To find out more about input devices, see Chapter 5.

Sensors can replace the need for a human to detect and record these changes. As it is a device and not a human doing this it may be less prone to error and natural variance in results. Sensors can also be used in situations to collect data where it is too dangerous for a human to work.

There are many different kinds of sensor that record data about many different aspects of the environment.

KEY TERM

Sensor – a type of input device that detects changes in the environment surround it.
Ambient light – the brightness or darkness at the current time.

6.02 Light sensors

A light sensor is a device that detects light. It will detect the **ambient light** level, meaning how bright or dark it is. In this way light sensors are like our eyes: we can detect how bright or dark it is and respond to this. We may put on sunglasses if we think it is too bright or we may switch on a lamp if we think it is too dark.

Light sensors can be used in street lights. We could set our street lights to turn on at a certain time each evening and turn off at a certain time each morning. However, the rate at which it gets dark each evening and light each morning changes throughout the year, even from day to day. This would mean we would regularly need to change the time we have set the street lights to turn on and off again. This could also mean that electricity is wasted if we get a particularly light evening and the street lights are turned on whilst it is still light. We could put a light sensor in street lamps to measure the ambient light level. When it gets too dark the lights will be automatically turned on and automatically turned off when it becomes light again.

Light sensors are used in many different ways and are built into many of the devices and systems we use on a daily basis. A security system can make use of light sensors. The sensors can beam light from one sensor to another. If a beam of light is broken by a person or object going through it, the next sensor will recognise this and send a signal to a computer to tell it the security system has been breached. This could then cause a response such as an alarm to sound. You may have seen an example of this kind of security system guarding precious items in movies.

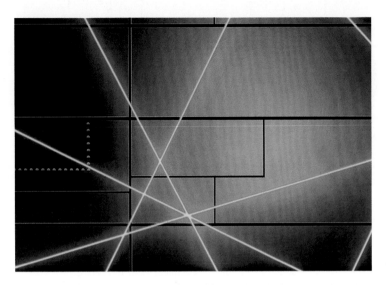

Figure 6.01 Light beams and light sensors can be used to create a security system

A light sensor can be used in regular devices in our household. We may have a garage door that opens and closes at the push of a button. However, if the button to close the garage door gets pushed accidentally, when a car or another item is in the way, there could be a lot of damage done. A beam of light can be sent from sensors lining the doorway that can check if anything is in the way. If the beam gets from one side to the other without being interrupted then the garage door can be triggered to close safely. Otherwise, if the beam is interrupted then the garage door can be stopped from closing to prevent any accidental damage.

Light sensors can be used in mobile phones for various different purposes. We can set the brightness of our screen to react to the ambient light around us. A light sensor will detect how bright or dark it is at the time and adjust the brightness of the mobile phone screen accordingly.

Other input devices that use light sensors are barcode and QR code scanners. These types of scanner shine light on the barcode or QR code. The light will then reflect back to the device. The white areas of the code will reflect more light than the black areas. The scanner will then convert the light reflections and create a series of binary digits that can be read by a computer.

Figure 6.02 Light beams and light sensors are used to read barcodes

Light sensors are used in many developing technologies such as robots. Light sensors can give the robot the ability to 'see'. Whist navigating around a room a robot could be constantly beaming light from itself. When the light beam bounces back more quickly, the robot will know that it is close to an object and can change direction.

Design a security system for your household that uses light sensors. What kind of things will you need to consider?

6.03 Temperature sensors

A temperature sensor is a device that measures heat generated by an object or system. By measuring the change in heat, the sensor can detect changes in temperature.

A temperature sensor will normally be one of two types, contact sensors and non-contact sensors. Contact temperature sensors need to have actual physical contact with an object to measure its temperature. The object could be solid, liquid or gas. A non-contact temperature sensor measures energy that is transmitted or radiated from an object.

Many household items use temperature sensors to regulate their temperature. We normally set our refrigerator to be at a constant certain temperature, for example 5 °C. The temperature conditions surrounding our refrigerator will be constantly changing and will affect the temperature inside. Also the temperature inside the refrigerator will be affected by opening the door to get things out of it. A temperature sensor will take regular samples of the temperature inside the refrigerator and adjust the temperature to keep it at a constant level. A temperature sensor in an oven will do the same thing to keep it at the temperature set.

A heating system in our household uses a particular kind of temperature sensor called a **thermostat**. On a very basic level a thermostat has two pieces of metal that will close together or open up depending on the current temperature. When the pieces of metal close together a circuit is created and electrical current will flow to heat up or cool down the atmosphere. If the atmosphere is at the correct temperature the metals will not touch and the circuit is broken to stop any electrical current flowing.

KEY TERM

Thermostat – a device that keeps temperature at a consistent level.

Figure 6.03 A thermostat can be used to control the temperature in a home or work place

Another sensor that measures temperature is an infrared sensor. Infrared sensors detect infrared radiation that emits from a person or object. Infrared waves are emitted by many things but they cannot be seen by the human eye.

We can use an infrared sensor to control our television. A television has an infrared sensor that will detect infrared waves from a remote control. A signal to change the channel or volume on the television can be sent as an infrared wave. The sensor will then interpret the signal and pass on the instruction to the television.

Infrared sensors can be used in a special kind of camera. The infrared camera will detect infrared waves being radiated by a person or object. This kind of technology can be used in many ways. It can be used when pursuing a criminal on the run from their crime. An infrared camera used from a helicopter will detect heat from a person. This way law enforcement can see if a criminal is hiding in, for example, a bush. A person will radiate more heat than a bush, so their shape will be able to be identified in the bush.

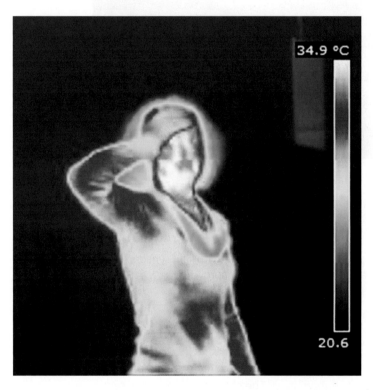

Figure 6.04 An example of infrared waves radiated by a human, taken by an infrared camera

Infrared cameras can also be used to measure the temperature of many things. For example, they are used in Formula 1 racing to show how hot the tyres on a car are. This allows a team to see if their current set of tyres is too hot. A viewer is often shown this image too in the television coverage and this can make interesting viewing for fans.

Infrared sensors can be used in security systems along with, or in place of, light sensors. They will detect the heat of a human and can trigger an alarm when this occurs.

Infrared technology is used in many other areas. It is used in astronomy to view objects in the universe that cannot be detected through the use of a normal camera. Most objects in the universe, such as stars, radiate infrared waves. These waves cannot be seen by the human eye, but when using a telescope they can be seen, allowing us to view the beauty of the sky. Aerospace engineers can also use infrared technology, to monitor the heat of an aeroplane in flight to see if any areas are in particular stress and at risk of damage.

Figure 6.05 Infrared technology can be used to take detailed astronomy images

TEST YOURSELF

Add infrared sensors to the security system you designed for your home with light sensors. How will the introduction of infrared sensors into the security system improve it?

6.04 Motion sensors

A motion sensor detects movement. They are also known as motion detectors. One of the most common uses of motion sensors is in a security system. The motion sensor will detect the movement of an intruder and can sound an alarm when this occurs. Motion can be detected in different ways. The two main ways are through detecting heat (this would use infrared technology) or by sending out microwaves that bounce off objects and would detect a change in the usual pattern if a moving object were to interrupt them.

Motion sensors can be used in lighting rooms in a business or even a household. Businesses have started using motion sensors to detect when a person walks into a room so that the lights are turned on when they do. Once the sensor stops detecting motion in the room it will automatically switch the lights off. This can help save energy and also money for the business as lights are only turned on when they are needed and are not left on in a room wasting energy.

Motion sensors can also be used in automatic doors. The sensor will detect when a person is approaching and open the doors in time for them to walk through. This can be a great benefit for people with disabilities who may struggle to open a door with ease. Allowing a door to automatically open so they can pass through can improve their access to many businesses, for example retail stores.

A developing use of motion sensors is in gaming. Motion sensors allow a person to interact with a game using the movement of their body. The first system to create this kind of gaming experience was the Nintendo Wii in 2006. Both Sony and Microsoft now have their own versions of movement-controlled gaming, Microsoft using a device called the Kinect and Sony using a device called the Move. The controller for the Nintendo Wii makes use of a particular kind of motion sensor called an **accelerometer**. This kind of motion sensor will detect any rotation, tilting and direction of the remote and communicates this to the computer system. This kind of sensor is also used in mobile phones and tablets to rotate the screen depending on the angle at which the user is holding the device.

KEY TERM

Accelerometer – a device that detects rotation and tilt.

Figure 6.06 Accelerometers can be used in a remote to detect different types of motion

6.05 Magnetic field sensors

Magnetic sensors detect changes in magnetic fields. They measure the strength and direction of a magnetic field and respond to its changes. The earth itself has a magnetic field and magnetic field sensors can be used to detect where north, south, east and west are. These kinds of sensor exist in our mobile phones and are called 'magnetometers'; they allow an application on our phone to act as a compass for us.

Magnetic sensors in a mobile phone could also be used to 'wake up' the phone by turning the screen on. A magnet can be placed inside the cover of a mobile phone case. When the magnetic field sensor detects the magnet is close by, the mobile phone screen will turn off as it will assume the cover is closed. When the magnetic field gets weaker as the cover is opened and moved away from direct contact with the mobile phone, the screen will turn on. This kind of technology can also be used in tablet computers.

6.06 Gas sensors

A gas sensor detects the presence of gas in a certain area and can trigger a response if the amount gets too high or too low.

Gas sensors are often used to detect the presence of carbon monoxide in our home, business or larger area. A carbon monoxide detector, that contains a gas sensor, can be placed in the rooms of a household or business that makes use of a gas central-heating system or gas fireplace. They will measure the level of carbon monoxide in the room and trigger an alarm or warning when the level gets too high. This is extremely important as humans can suffer from carbon monoxide poisoning that can be fatal to us if we are exposed to too much.

Gas detectors can be used in many areas of industry. They can be used in a nuclear energy plant to detect any gases that could cause fire and a potentially critical situation. They can also be used in waste water treatment plants to detect any toxic gases that may be present when trying to purify the water.

TEST YOURSELF

Can you think of any other industries where the detection of gas could be vital?

6.07 Pressure sensors

A pressure sensor measures the pressure of a liquid or a gas. Lots of pressure sensors are used in our daily lives to measure the pressure of liquid flowing through pipes. It is extremely important for the pressure of such things to be measured as if too much liquid is flowing through a pipe it may burst.

Pressure is measured by causing a certain material used in the area, for example inside the pipe, to conduct electricity at a certain rate. The level will be matched to a set level of pressure that can be monitored. If more liquid flows through, causing too much pressure, the level of electricity conducted will increase and this can trigger a warning of too much pressure occurring in that area.

6.08 Moisture and humidity sensors

A moisture sensor measures the amount of moisture in a certain material whereas a humidity sensor measures the amount of moisture in the air, along with its temperature.

The most common use of a moisture sensor is in detecting the moisture levels in soil. Getting the correct level of moisture into soil is vital when farming crops. In order to get the best quality crop, a farmer would benefit from measuring the level of moisture in the soil on their land. This way they can keep it at a constant level and the best level to get the highest quality crop. Through measuring the moisture in the soil, a farmer can create an **automated** system that will water the crop automatically when the moisture levels of the soil get too low. It will also alert them when the water levels become too high so that action can be taken to make sure the crop is not ruined.

 KEY TERM

Automated – a process that is automatic.

92

Another name for a humidity sensor is a hygrometer. They measure the amount of water vapour present in the air and the current temperature of the air. The two of these measures together are known as humidity. There can be many reason why a person would need to measure the humidity of air. A person who has an illness or a condition that can be affected by humidity may have a humidity sensor in their home. High humidity can cause the growth of bacteria that can affect health and, with certain illnesses, if the air gets too dry this can cause them to have problems with their breathing.

Humidity sensors can also be used in places such as museums and art galleries. It may be damaging to certain artefacts and paintings if the air is too humid, so it needs to be monitored to make sure that this doesn't happen.

6.09 pH sensors

A pH sensor measures how acidic or alkaline a material is. The pH is measured on a scale. The value 7 of a pH scale means a material is pH neutral. A pH of less than 7 indicates a material is acidic and a pH of more than 7 indicates a material is alkaline.

It is extremely important that the pH is correct for the water that we drink in order for us to remain healthy. The pH of the most pure water would be 7, so most water treatment plants will try and get as close as possible to this. A water treatment plant will measure the pH of the water that it holds to make sure that it does not become too acidic or too alkaline. It could be very damaging to their reputation if they were to risk this happening.

The level of pH in water is also monitored in aquariums, the tanks that fish are kept in. It is important for the pH level to be set at a certain point for different types of fish. It is even more important that the pH level remains consistent; any changes could be fatal for the fish.

93

Summary

- A sensor is a type of input device.

- There are many different kinds of sensors that record data about many different aspects of the environment.

- A light sensor is a device that detects light. It will detect the ambient light level, meaning how bright or dark it is.

- A temperature sensor is a device that measures heat generated by an object or system. By measuring the change in heat, the sensor can detect any changes in temperature.

- Another sensor that measures temperature is an infrared sensor. Infrared sensors detect infrared radiation that emits from a person or object.

- A motion sensor detects movement.

- Magnetic sensors detect changes in magnetic fields. It will measure the strength and direction of a magnetic field and respond to its changes.

- A gas sensor detects the presence of gas in a certain area. It measures the amount of gas in certain area and can trigger a response if the amount gets too high or too low.

- A pressure sensor measures pressure. Lots of pressure sensors are used in our daily lives to measure the pressure of liquid flowing through pipes.

- Moisture sensors measure the amount of moisture in a certain material whereas a humidity sensor measures the amount of moisture in the air, along with its temperature.

- A PH sensor measures how acidic or alkaline a material is.

Exam-style questions

1   Define the term 'sensor'.   (1 mark)

2   Identify three different sensors that could be used to increase safety in a   (3 marks)
    nuclear plant and describe how they would do this.

3   Explain two drawbacks of using motion sensors in a security system and   (4 marks)
    suggest how they could be overcome.

4   Explain how the use of moisture sensors can improve farming.   (3 marks)

5   Describe how an infrared sensor works.   (2 marks)

6   Describe how a light sensor is used to read a barcode.   (4 marks)

Chapter 7:
Output Devices

Learning objectives

By the end of this chapter you will:

- understand what an output device is and why they are necessary
- understand that different output devices output different forms of information, such as text, images, sound and movement
- understand how flat-panel display screens, liquid crystal display (LCD) and light-emitting diode (LED) screens, touch screens, LCD projectors and Digital light projectors (DLP) operate
- understand what is meant by a printer and a cutter and how different printers and cutters operate
- understand what is meant by speakers and headphones and how they operate
- understand what is meant by an actuator and how they operate.

7.01 Introduction

The function of a computer is to input data, process it and output the resulting information. An output device is a **peripheral** that is used to output information.

Information can be output in many different forms. When designing a computer system we need to know what information it will output, how the output will be presented and the best way to achieve this. Different types of output device exist and they output information in a different way.

The first outputs from computers were cards with holes punched into them. The pattern in which the holes were punched represented the data. Today, the most common forms of output are **soft copies** from displays, **hard copies** from printers and sound from speakers and headphones.

All output devices take up space on a desk, in a cupboard or on the floor. The space taken by a peripheral is called its **footprint**.

KEY TERM

Peripheral – an external device that is connected to a computer.
Soft copy – data and information that is virtual.
Hard copy – data and information that is physical.
Footprint – the space taken up by a peripheral.

96

TEST YOURSELF

1   How many output devices can you see in your classroom?
2   Do the output devices produce soft copies or hard copies of data?

7.02 Displays

SYLLABUS CHECK

Describe the principles of operation of the following output devices: flat-panel display screens, including Liquid Crystal Display (LCD) and Light-Emitting Diodes (LED); LCD projectors and Digital Light Projectors (DLP).
Describe how these principles are applied to real-life scenarios.

A display is an electronic device that outputs information via a screen or projection. This information can be in the form of text, images or video. As most modern computers, such as laptops, tablets and smartphones, contain a built-in screen, displays are considered to be the most immediate form of output. An external display, for example one used with a desktop PC, is often referred to as a monitor or visual display unit (VDU).

KEY TERM

Pixel – short for picture element; it is an illuminated dot; many pixels together form an image.
Resolution – the number of pixels in a display.

The image on a display is built up of thousands of tiny illuminated dots called **pixels**, short for picture elements. The quality of the image depends on the **resolution** of the display. The resolution of a display is the amount of pixels the display contains. Different screens have different resolutions and larger displays will normally have more pixels. The higher the number of pixels, the higher the resolution of the display, as in Table 7.01.

Table 7.01

Screen type	Resolution (pixels)	Number of pixels
Typical smartphone	800 × 480	84 000
Typical tablet	1280 × 800	1 024 000
Typical 13-inch laptop	1280 × 800	1 024 000
Typical 19-inch desktop PC	1440 × 900	1 296 000
22-inch screen	1920 × 1080	2 073 600
Typical projector	1024 × 768	786 432
Standard-definition TV	1280 × 720	921 600
High-definition TV	1920 × 1080	2 073 600
4k TV	3840 × 2160	8 294 400

A display with a small number of pixels is known as a low-resolution display. A display with a large number of pixels is known as a high-resolution display. Low-resolution displays are suitable when a high level of detail is not necessary, such as displaying text. High-resolution displays provide a clear, detailed image and are required when a high level of detail is essential, such as image editing, video production and graphic design.

Displays produce either monochrome or colour images. Monochrome images have two colours: one foreground colour and one background colour. The two colours are normally black and white. Colour displays produce images by combining the three primary colours: red, green and blue (RGB). Different mixtures and strengths of these primary colours can be combined to create different shades of colour.

Displays have a colour depth. This is the degree to which a particular colour can be represented, for example how bright or pale a colour is. Colour depth is represented as series of bits. The more bits, the greater the colour depth and the closer to a particular shade of colour the display can produce. The higher the number of bits, the greater the number of possible colour shades as in Table 7.02.

Table 7.02

Colour depth	Allows
1-bit monochrome	2 colours – primarily black and white, however, any two colours can be used
8-bit grayscale	256 shades, running from solid white to solid black
8-bit colour	256 colours
16-bit colour (also known as high colour)	65 536 colours
24-bit colour (also known as true colour)	16 777 216 colours
30, 36 or 48-bit colour (also known as deep colour)	Billions of colours

Modern displays commonly offer 24-bit colour, although some smartphones and tablets are restricted to 16-bit colour.

To learn more about pixels and resolution, see Chapter 1.

Displays can be portrait or landscape in orientation:

- Portrait displays are squarer in nature. They have a ratio of width to height of 4:3. Older televisions and monitors normally have a portrait display.
- Landscape displays are rectangular in nature. They have a ratio of width to height of 16:9. Modern televisions and computers, tablets and smartphone displays tend to have landscape screens. Landscape displays are also called widescreen displays.

Some devices, such as tablets and smartphones, have the ability to switch the display between portrait and landscape modes:

- Portrait mode offers more height. It is best suited to viewing documents where the content runs in columns, such as a page of a book or an article.
- Landscape mode offers more width. It is best suited to viewing images and videos.

The size of a display is usually measured from one corner to the diagonally opposite corner, and not its height or width. Therefore, a 22-inch display measures 22 inches from the top left corner to bottom right corner.

Flat-panel displays

For many years the most common form of display was the cathode ray tube (CRT) display. A CRT consists of a sealed glass tube with a fluorescent coating of phosphor dots applied to the inside. Colours are created by mixing various shades of the basic RGB colours. Electrons fired at the tube by three separate electron guns (one each for RGB colour) illuminate the fluorescent coating to create an image. These displays are limited in resolution, bulky in size and use a lot of energy. They also produce flickering images that can strain your eyes.

Today, CRTs have been largely replaced by flat-panel displays. Flat-panel displays are thinner in depth, lighter and use less energy compared with CRTs. They also provide higher resolution, brighter, flicker-free images. Flat-panel displays do have their drawbacks. They are easily damaged if dropped. This means that many people damage the screen on their smartphone or tablet. They can also suffer from 'dead pixels'. This is where a pixel remains constantly illuminated no matter what image is displayed. This degrades the picture. As well as computer monitors, flat-panel displays are ideal for use in devices where size and energy use is important, for example laptops, mobile phones, tablets and digital cameras.

Table 7.03

Advantages of flat-panel displays	Disadvantages of flat-panel displays
They have a high-resolution, bright, flicker-free image. This increases the detail of text, images and video	They can be easily damaged if dropped
They can be made at a size ideal for a portable device	They can suffer from dead pixels that will spoil the display
They have low energy requirements. This is ideal for use with battery-powered devices	

Figure 7.01 Flat-panel displays are thinner, lighter and use less energy than previous types of display

Flat-panel displays come in two main formats: liquid crystal displays (LCD) and light-emitting diode (LED) displays.

Liquid crystal display (LCD)

A liquid crystal display (LCD) is made up of separate red, green and blue coloured pixels arranged together in tiny blocks. Each block is made up of liquid crystals. The crystals can be made to turn solid or transparent by altering the electric current that is supplied to the block. A backlight made up of cold cathode fluorescent lamps (CCFL), similar in nature to fluorescent tubes used in room lighting, shines light behind the pixels. When the crystal is transparent, light is let through and the pixels are illuminated. When the crystal is solid, the pixels remain dark. Colour is created by illuminating sufficient red, green and blue pixels to achieve the desired shade.

LCD displays are thin in size and do not use a lot of energy. This makes them ideal for portable devices such as laptops, tablets, smartphones, PDAs and in-car satellite navigation systems. Additionally, LCDs do not damage our eyes as much because they do not produce glare. However, unless viewed straight on, the image displayed on a LCD can be hard to see.

Light-emitting diode (LED) display

The light-emitting diode (LED) display is a more advanced version of the liquid crystal display. An LED display works the same way as an LCD except that the pixels are backlit with light-emitting diodes. LEDs produce a brighter, more direct light. They are smaller and thinner than the cathode lamps used by LCDs. This means that LED displays can be made thinner and lighter than the equivalent LCDs. The image is also visible over a wider viewing angle.

However, LED screens sometimes suffer from uneven brightness across the display. This happens more with large displays. LED displays can be less energy efficient than LCDs. Although individual LEDs require very little energy, the large numbers required to light a large display can mean more energy is used.

TEST YOURSELF

Another type of LED display is the OLED display. Research OLED technology and find out what advantages OLED offers over LED.

7.03 Digital projectors

A digital projector is a display device connected to a computer that is used to project digital video output onto a flat area such as a wall, projector screen or interactive whiteboard.

To learn more about interactive whiteboards, see Chapter 5.

Projectors are used when an output needs to be shown on a large scale, for example a presentation to a large audience. Due to the nature of light projection, the further away the projector is from the wall or screen, the larger the image. This means that projectors are useful where information needs be presented to large numbers of people, such as in business meetings, classrooms and at conferences. However, the greater the distance, the dimmer the image will be as the projected light is spread.

There are two main types of projector to consider: the liquid crystal display (LCD) projector and the digital light processing (DLP) projector.

Figure 7.02 Digital projectors can be used to present information to a large number of people

LCD projector

An LCD projector contains three separate LCD glass panels, one for each of the RGB colours in an image. As the light passes through the LCD panels, individual pixels can be opened, to allow light to pass, or closed, to block the light. LCD projectors are useful when contrast and brightness is important.

DLP projector

A DLP projector uses millions of tiny mirrors to reflect light towards the projection lens. This system creates an image with excellent colour reproduction, but one that has less contrast and brightness. As they have fewer internal components, DLP projectors are smaller. This makes them more portable than their LCD equivalents.

7.04 Printers

SYLLABUS CHECK

Describe the principles of operation of the following output devices: inkjet, laser and 3D printers; 2D and 3D cutters; speakers and headphones; actuators.

Describe how these principles are applied to real-life scenarios.

Printers are devices that produce hard copies of information. A hard copy is a physical copy, for example a printout of a typed document or an image. Printouts are made so that users can take a copy of information away to look at, share with others or keep as a permanent record.

Some printers produce monochrome printouts, usually in black and white. Other printers produce colour printouts. However, unlike displays that form all colours from RGB, printers create colours from three base colours: cyan (C), magenta (M) and yellow (Y). To give definition and clarity to the image, black is also used. This is called the key (K). Together these four colours are known as CMYK. Printers create images using ink or toner. CMYK ink or toner colours are mixed together at varying strengths to form different colours. CMY are lighter colours. Mixing them together will produce darker colours. As they are light colours to start with, it takes a lot of ink or toner to achieve much darker colours. The colours RGB are darker colours, a different mixture of them is needed to create colours than is needed for CMYK. This means that colours shown on a printed document will appear different to those presented on a display.

Printers form images by printing tiny dots. Print resolution is measured in **dots per inch (DPI)**. The more dots printed per inch, the higher the resolution. As with displays, printers are available with differing print resolutions. 300 DPI is considered high resolution for a printer. Resolutions of 150 to 200 DPI are suitable for most purposes. Printers can print in many different paper sizes. The footprint of a printer varies according to the size of paper it can print on to.

KEY TERM

Dots-per-inch (DPI) – the resolution of a printed image.

Figure 7.03 Printers use a mixture of cyan, magenta, yellow and key (black) to create different colours

Several types of printer exist and each type produces hard copies in a different way. As a result, some printers are more suitable for certain situations. Printer types include:

- inkjet printer
- laser printer
- three-dimensional (3D) printer.

Inkjet printers

An inkjet printer uses ink to print information. The ink is provided in a cartridge and is sprayed through microscopic nozzles onto paper. Colour inkjet printers often have four cartridges, one for each CMYK colour.

Inkjet technology is relatively cheap, making inkjet printers a popular choice for home use. However, as paper absorbs ink, definition is not always particularly sharp. Ink absorption also prevents printing on both sides of the page, as the image printed on one side may show through to the other. This is known as 'see through'. Definition can be increased if photographic paper is used. This is because ink will not be absorbed in the same way.

Inkjet printers are slow to produce copies. They are usually capable of printing around 5–15 pages per minute. Although inkjet cartridges are cheap, they run out of ink quickly as they need to use a lot of ink. The nozzles can also clog making the cartridge useless. As a result, they are best suited to situations where low levels of printing are required and quality is of less importance. Inkjet printers do produce superior colour to laser printers. This means they are more suitable for printing photographs.

Table 7.04

Advantages of inkjet printers	Disadvantages of inkjet printers
They are cheaper to buy than most other printers	They are expensive to run as they can use a lot of ink, which is expensive to buy
Image quality can be excellent when used with photographic paper	Image quality can be poor when printing on ordinary paper
	It is difficult to print on both sides of paper
	They are slow at printing

Laser printers

A laser printer uses a special powder called toner to print out information. The toner is provided in a cartridge. As with colour inkjet printers, colour laser printers normally have four cartridges, one for each CMYK colour.

Laser printers use a laser to create static electricity on certain areas of the page. These areas correspond to the image or text that is being printed. Toner is then scattered onto the page. The static electricity attracts the toner and causes it to stick to the page. This forms the image or text to be output. Finally, a fusing element makes sure the toner is bonded to the page.

Laser technology is more expensive to buy. This makes laser printers a less popular choice for home use as they are more expensive. Laser printers also tend to have a larger footprint than inkjet printers. However, as toner is not absorbed into paper, the quality of printed text is higher as it is sharper. Laser printers are capable of printing much faster than inkjet printers. They can print up to 60 pages per minute. Although toner cartridges are more expensive than ink cartridges, they last longer and allow many more copies to be printed. Many laser printers also allow double sided printing (duplex printing), this reduces paper costs. As a result, laser printers are extremely well suited to business use, where cheap, high-speed printing is desirable.

Table 7.05

Advantages of laser printers	Disadvantages of laser printers
They are cheap to run as toner cartridges last much longer	They are expensive to buy as laser technology is expensive
Text printing quality is generally excellent	Image printing quality on photographic paper is not as good as an inkjet printer
They are very quick at printing	They normally have a larger footprint than an equivalent inkjet printer
They are suitable for duplex printing. This reduces paper costs	

TEST YOURSELF

Determine which type of printer would be best suited to these applications and explain why:
- a family wanting to print copies of digital photos
- an accountant wanting to print monthly budget spreadsheets
- a small business wanting to print invoices.

Three-dimensional (3D) printer

3D printing is the process of creating three-dimensional objects. A 3D printer is a device that outputs the 3D objects.

The 3D printing process requires an object to first be drawn up as a 3D model in a digital file. The object can be created using either a **computer-aided design (CAD)** application or by scanning an object with a 3D scanner. The digital object is then split into thousands of extremely thin, horizontal layers. Starting at the bottom, the 3D printer uses a material such as polymers, acrylic or plastic to slowly print each individual layer, one on top of another. 3D printing is also known as additive manufacturing. This is because during the printing process the printed object is added to layer by layer.

 KEY TERM

Computer-aided design (CAD) – software that allows a user to design and create an image of an object.

To learn more about 3D scanners, see Chapter 5.

Figure 7.04 3D printers create objects by printing horizontal layers of material, one on top of the other

3D printers are not designed for mass production of objects. They are more suitable for creating individual items. The process allows an engineer to quickly build and test an object design without having to wait for a prototype to be manufactured. They can also be used to produce bespoke items fairly quickly. 3D printing technology is expensive but it has become much more affordable. This has meant some schools, small businesses and homes now have 3D printers.

3D printers can be used in many ways:

- In China, a large-scale 3D printer was used to print a five-storey apartment building.
- Astronauts on the International Space Station have printed tools.
- People who make models can print replacement parts for broken or missing pieces.
- Archaeologists and palaeontologists have printed replicas of ancient objects such as fossils.
- In the United Kingdom, students at Sheffield University used a 3D printer to print bespoke parts to build a telescope that took images using a Raspberry Pi.

3D printing can have issues as well as benefits. The materials used to printed objects may not be as strong or as durable as traditionally manufactured items. 3D printers can also allow the creation of dangerous items such as weapons, making these items accessible to anyone who has access to the design and a 3D printer. Copyright issues could also exist if users replicate and print a copyrighted design.

Table 7.06

Advantages of 3D printers	Disadvantages of 3D printers
Bespoke items or prototypes can be made quickly	3D printing is quite expensive
Just about any shape can be printed	Printed items might not be as durable as a similar manufactured product
Costs to a designer can be reduced as they can easily change a design, re-print it and test it without having to have the object manufactured	Dangerous items may be printed
Designs can easily be shared by sharing the digital file	Copyright issues may exist if a copyrighted design is printed

7.05 Computer-aided manufacturing (CAM)

Computer-aided manufacturing (CAM) is a process where computers and machinery work together to manufacture products. CAM uses computer-aided design (CAD) software to design a product. Additional software then takes the design and controls machine tools to create the product. First, a workflow is determined by the user. This dictates which machine tools are to be used and when. The CAM software then controls and monitors the machine tools to make sure the product is manufactured correctly.

KEY TERM

Computer-aided manufacturing (CAM) – a computer controls machinery to manufacture an object.
Computer-numerical control (CNC) – the method of control used by CAM.

Machine tools involved in CAM include lathes, cutters, drills and conveyors. CAM software works by issuing a series of numbers to the machine tools it controls. The numbers are information the machine needs.

- A cutting machine needs to know what depth the material needs to be cut and at what angle.

- A conveyor needs to know what speed the material needs to be moved along the belt.

- A drill needs to know what depth a hole needs to be drilled and what speed to operate at.

Controlling machines using numbers is known as **computer numerical control (CNC)**. CNC allows precision manufacturing that is more accurate than we can achieve by hand. Once a machine has been programmed and controlled using CNC, many items can be manufactured. High-quality bespoke items and prototypes can also be produced.

CAM requires training. Engineers need to understand how machinery works, how to control the machinery using numbers and how to design a workflow to manufacture the product. CAM is expensive to introduce, but once set up can be cheaper to run than employing a workforce.

Table 7.07

Advantages of CAM	Disadvantages of CAM
Items can be manufactured to a higher precision than by hand	Training is required to use CAM
High production quality can be maintained when making many products	Bespoke items and prototypes may be expensive to produce
It can produce high-quality bespoke items and prototypes	CAM is expensive to introduce because of the hardware and software costs involved

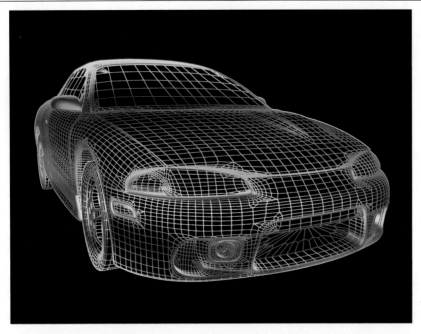

Figure 7.05 CAD software can be used to design many products

Figure 7.06 CAD can be used in CAM to create the product

2-dimensional (2D) CAM machines

2D CAM machines are also known as 'cutters'. They manipulate materials in two dimensions. Various types of cutter exist, for example blade, laser and water jet cutters. Cutters vary in size and the size of the cutter determines the size of the material that can be cut.

- Blade cutters use a blade to cut and trim materials such as paper, card and vinyl. They are often used to create signs and some advertising materials, for example billboards. Blade cutters are cheaper than other types of cutter. They can be noisy.

- Laser cutters use a laser to cut or etch into materials. They are typically used for industrial manufacturing. A high-powered laser enables precise shapes to be cut out of sheets or blocks. The excess material after the shape has been cut is drawn out of the machine by an extractor. 2D laser cutters can cut a variety of materials such as wood, plastic, metal and textiles. Lasers can also allow designs to be etched into materials as well as cutting them. Laser cutters are quick, accurate and quiet.

- Water jet cutters use a pressurised stream of water mixed with an abrasive element. The abrasive element that is used in most water cutters is the gem stone garnet. These types of cutter enable precision cutting of polished and reflective materials, for example a mirror, without spoiling the materials coating or finish.

3-dimensional (3D) cutters

2D CAM machines only allow cutting in two dimensions. 3D machines such as millers or routers have tools that rotate on six axes. This means a shape can be cut in 3 dimensions. 3D cutters are commonly used for cutting wood, MDF, wax, plastics and acrylics. As well as producing bespoke products, they are used to test and modify prototype designs. This helps reduce errors whilst saving time and money.

Although different in nature, 3D cutters and 3D printers produce similar final products.

7.06 Speakers and headphones

Speakers are a device used to output sound. For sound to be output, the digital sound file needs to be converted to an analogue signal via the use of a **digital-to-analogue convertor (DAC).** This is usually in the form of a sound card. The speaker translates this signal into a sound wave by moving a cone to vibrate air.

 KEY TERM

Digital-to-analogue convertor (DAC) – a device that converts digital signals to analogue.

To learn more about analogue signals see Chapter 1.

Speakers can be used to output sound for many different purposes, including:

- listening to music for entertainment
- alerting us to a message or reminder
- giving feedback to a user to tell them an action has been carried out
- as an alarm to warn of an intruder
- to aid a disabled person in completing tasks.

Figure 7.07 A speaker translates an analogue signal into a sound wave by moving a cone to vibrate air

Many devices, such as laptops, tablets, smartphones and televisions have built-in speakers. The quality of these devices is generally fairly low. Higher quality external speakers are available that give a much higher quality sound reproduction. Devices without internal speakers, for example a desktop PC, often have a sound card with a socket to connect speakers.

Speakers are useful but the sound output they produce can disturb other users. Headphones can be used in place of speakers so that only one person can hear the output. Headphones contain a small pair of speakers that cover the ear, sending sound only towards the ear.

Table 7.08

Advantages of speakers	Disadvantages of speakers
They allow a variety of information to be provided to the user	Built-in speakers often give low quality sound reproduction
They can aid a disabled user when operating a device	The sound produced may disturb other users
They are useful to warn a large amount of people at once about an emergency	A sound card with a digital-to-analogue convertor is needed to convert information to a form a speaker can output

7.07 Actuators

Sometimes outputs can be a movement or an action. An actuator is a mechanical output device that produces movement. The moving part of an actuator is usually connected to another device in order to move that device. Actuators can rotate, open, close, push and pull an object. They apply movement through the use of energy and the energy is converted into motion.

Actuators are used for tasks such as:

- controlling a robotic arm
- spinning a fan
- pumping water.

109

Figure 7.08 Actuators are used to produce the movement of a robot arm

TEST YOURSELF

Think of a device that may use an actuator in your home?

Summary

- Computers need to be able to output information. Information can take the form of text, images, video, sound or action.

- Output devices are peripherals that allow information to be output.

- A display is an electronic device that outputs information via a screen or projection.

- Flat-panel displays are thin in depth and are fairly lightweight. Flat-panel displays are ideal for use in devices where size and energy use are important, such as laptops, mobile phones and digital cameras.

- LCDs consist of separate red, green and blue coloured pixels arranged together in tiny blocks. LCDs are ideal for portable devices such as laptops, tablets, smartphones, PDAs and in-car satellite navigation systems.

- LED displays are a more advanced version of LCDs. They work in the same way except that the pixels are backlit with LEDs, which produce brighter displays.

- A digital projector is a display device connected to a computer that is used to project digital video output onto a flat area such as a wall, projector screen or interactive whiteboard.

- A printer is a device for outputting hard copies of information.

- 3D printers print solid objects. They are not designed for mass production of objects, but more for creating individual items.

- CAM is a process where computers and machinery perform together to manufacture products. CAM utilises 2D and 3D cutters.

- Speakers are a sound outputting device. For sound to be output, the digital sound file needs to be converted to an analogue signal via the use of a DAC.

- An actuator is a mechanical output device that produces movement.

Exam-style questions

1   Explain what is meant by an output device.   (2 marks)

2   Explain why LCD screens are more suited to portable devices than CRTs.   (2 marks)

3   Explain why printers do not print in RGB.   (2 marks)

4   Vikram wants a new printer to take to university. He will be printing mainly   (2 marks)
    essays and reports. State which type of printer would be most suitable and
    say why.

5   Explain what is meant by the resolution of a display.   (3 marks)

6   Discuss how and why 3D printing may become a more common technology   (4 marks)
    in the home.

Chapter 8:
Memory, Storage Devices and Media

Learning objectives

By the end of this chapter you will:

- understand what is meant by primary, secondary and off-line storage
- know that primary storage is Read Only Memory (ROM) and Random Access Memory (RAM)
- know that secondary storage is hard disk drives (HDD) and Solid State Drives (SSD)
- understand that off-line storage can be optical, magnetic or solid state
- understand the principles of operation of primary memory, secondary memory and off-line storage
- be able to describe how these principles are applied to currently available storage solutions such as HDDs, SSDs, USB flash memory, DVDs, CDs and Blu-ray disks.

8.01 Storage media

SYLLABUS CHECK

Show understanding of the difference between: primary, secondary and off-line storage.

In today's world we are used to having computers with a large storage capacity. Even smaller devices, such as smart phones and media players, usually have several gigabytes of data storage. However, it has taken a lot of development to get storage devices to be so small and have such a large capacity. The first storage device (a hard disk) to have a gigabyte of data was created in 1980 by IBM. It was as large as a refrigerator and cost over $80 000 USD.

Figure 8.01   The IBM 3380 was the first storage device to have a capacity of 1 gigabyte

As mentioned in previous chapters, the function of a computer is to input data, process it and output the resulting information. Data is held in storage for processing and so that it can be retrieved for later use.

There are three types of storage that a computer uses:

- primary storage
- secondary storage
- off-line storage

Primary storage

SYLLABUS CHECK

Provide examples of primary storage, such as: Read Only Memory (ROM) and Random Access Memory (RAM).

Primary storage is also known as 'primary memory' or 'memory'. Once data has been input into a computer, it needs to be stored in a place that can be accessed quickly and directly by the computer's processor. Primary storage is a computer's internal storage. It is in this storage where data is held ready for processing. Compared to secondary and off-line storage, the capacity of primary storage is quite small. Primary storage is separated into Random Access Memory (RAM) and Read Only Memory (ROM). Both types are memory chips.

Random Access Memory (RAM)

RAM is primary storage that holds data to be processed and programs that are in use. This means that RAM is storage that data can be written to and read from. Data and programs in RAM are held temporarily and erased when they are no longer needed. RAM also loses its contents when the computer's power is switched off. As a result we say that RAM is 'volatile'.

The amount of RAM built into a computer varies with the type of computer and its purpose. However, RAM can often be expanded to increase storage capacity. **Embedded computers** such as a pocket calculator, digital watch or central heating control system may only have a few kilobytes of RAM. This is because they only need to process small amounts of data at any one time. However, modern **general purpose computers**, such as desktop PCs, laptops, tablets and smartphones, will have a few gigabytes of RAM. This is because at any given time, the RAM in a general purpose computer will hold the operating system, programs that are currently running and data that is being processed.

RAM is often built into peripherals such as printers. Data to be printed is transferred to the printer's RAM, then the printer prints the data whilst the computer moves on to other tasks.

KEY TERM

Embedded computer – a computer that is built into a device and performs one or more specialised tasks.

General purpose computer – a computer used for many different applications.

TEST YOURSELF

Think of three other embedded computers in your school?

Read Only Memory (ROM)

ROM is primary storage that can be read from but not written to. Unlike RAM, ROM does not lose its contents when the computer's power is switched off. As a result we say that ROM is 'non-volatile'.

The contents of ROM vary depending on the type of device. Embedded devices use ROM to hold the software that runs the device. This software is known as **firmware**. General purpose devices use ROM to hold software known as a **bootstrap**. The bootstrap contains instructions that determine the basic hardware structure of the computer and instructions for finding and loading the operating system.

Certain types of ROM can be erased and re-written to. This type of ROM is known as **erasable programmable read only memory (EPROM)**. EPROM is found in situations where a device's firmware may need to be upgraded at some point in the future. For example, modern smart televisions, Blu-ray players and smartphones all have firmware that can be updated by the user. Upgrading firmware is known as **flashing**.

KEY TERM

Firmware – ROM that holds programs that run on an embedded computer.

Bootstrap – ROM that contains start-up instructions for the computer.

Erasable Programmable Read Only Memory (EPROM) – ROM that can be erased and re-written.

Flashing – the process of erasing and re-writing data to ROM.

Table 8.01

RAM	ROM
RAM is like a whiteboard. It can be written to, read from, erased, or left as it is. Its contents are temporary	ROM is like a book. Once written, it can usually only be read from. Its contents are mostly permanent
RAM is volatile. It loses its contents when power is switched off	ROM is non-volatile. It retains its contents when the power is switched off
In embedded devices, RAM holds data for processing. In general purpose computers, RAM hold the operating system, running programs and data for processing	ROM holds firmware and bootstraps
Depending on the device, RAM can range in capacity from a few bytes to several gigabytes	ROM tends to be much smaller in capacity

TEST YOURSELF

1   Research cache memory. What type of memory is it and why is it used?
2   Why does a computer need both RAM and ROM?

Secondary storage

SYLLABUS CHECK

Provide examples of secondary storage, such as: hard disk drive (HDD) and Solid State Drive (SSD).

114

Although general purpose computers have a large capacity of RAM, the storage requirements of data and software make it very impractical (and sometime impossible) to hold all necessary data and software in RAM at the same time. Software and data also need to be kept for future use, but are lost from RAM when the computer is switched off. Therefore we need secondary storage to hold data and software on a more permanent basis. They can be held in secondary storage until they are erased or over-written when no longer required. General purpose computers such as desktop PCs and laptops also use secondary storage to hold the operating system.

The CPU in a computer can only access data when it is being held in the RAM. Therefore, programs, data and an operating system must first be transferred into RAM from secondary storage before the processor can access them.

As secondary storage needs to hold large volumes of data and software, it is large in capacity, ranging in size from around 500 MB through to a terabyte, or more. Some secondary storage devices are removable. This means they can be transported between computers.

Table 8.02

Primary storage	Secondary storage
Directly accessible by the processor as it is internal to the computer	Not directly accessible to the processor – data first has to be transferred into RAM
Temporarily stores data	Permanently stores data till erased
Can be read from and written to primary storage almost instantly	Slower to read data from and write data to, as it needs to be transferred into RAM first
Normally a few gigabytes in capacity	Can be up to a terabyte or more in capacity
Fixed within the computer	Some devices are removable

There are three types of secondary storage that we need to consider:

- magnetic storage
- optical storage
- solid-state storage.

Each works in a different way and is used for a different purpose.

Magnetic storage

Magnetic storage devices read, write and erase data by using electromagnets and magnetic fields to control tiny magnetic dots of data. The dots represent binary.

Magnetic devices are either tape based or disk based. Tape-based devices use a cartridge of looped magnetic tape. The magnetised data dots are stored in series along the length of the tape. The tape passes over an electromagnetic read/write head that reads, writes or erases the magnetic dots.

Figure 8.02 The magnetised data dots are stored in series along the length of the magnetic tape

Disk-based devices, such as hard disk drives, consist of several disks known as platters. Platters can be made from metal or glass. They have a magnetised coating on which the data dots are stored. The dots lie in tracks that run around a platter. The platters are attached to a rotating spindle. This spindle spins the platters at high speed. Data is read, written or erased as the dots pass under read/write heads that sit on a moving arm. The arm moves back and forth across the platters to access data in different tracks.

Hard disk drives are the most common form of secondary storage device. They can hold up to 8 terabytes of data, although normally far less. A magnetic tape can hold up to 185 terabytes.

Figure 8.03 In a hard disk, an arm moves back and forth across platters to access data in different tracks

The rate at which data is moved to and from a storage device is called the 'data transfer rate'. Data is usually transferred much faster with a hard disk than with tape. Many modern hard disk drives have data transfer rates of up to 185 megabytes per second, whereas tape devices are usually limited to around 30 megabytes per second. This is partly because data can be read quicker using disk technology, but also because of the way data is stored and accessed on the two devices. Data is stored serially on magnetic tape. This means if the data required is near the point at which the tape starts being read, then the data will be quickly found and transferred. However, if the data is far away from that point, the tape has to loop around to the correct place first. Data on disks can be accessed directly as the read/write heads can move directly to the point at which the data is stored. This saves time and increases access speed.

To learn more about different types of data transfer, see Chapter 2.

TEST YOURSELF

Are there any computers in your school that use magnetic storage?

Optical storage

Optical storage devices read data by shining a laser beam onto the surface of plastic disks. The disks are coated with aluminium to make them reflective. The reflective surface is covered in one large track that spirals outwards from the centre of the disk. Data is written on the track by using a laser to make indentations known as **pits**. These pits represent binary data. The areas in between pits are known as **land**. As a pit reflects light back differently from land, the optical device is able to differentiate between binary 1s and 0s. For example, supposing we recorded the binary data 11101001. This would be recorded on the disk as:

Table 8.03

Disk	Pit			Land	Pit	Land		Pit
Binary Representation	1	1	1	0	1	0	0	1

The process of recording data onto an optical disk is known as 'burning'. This is because the laser burns the pits into the disk surface.

Optical disks have a good data transfer rate with speeds ranging between 10 and 72 megabytes per second. Newer formats, such as Blu-ray, are far quicker than older formats such as compact disk. There are different types of optical disk including **compact disks (CDs), digital versatile disks (DVDs)** and **Blu-ray disks**.

KEY TERM

Pit – an indentation on the surface of an optical disk, used to represent data.

Land – the raised surface between pits on an optical disk.

Compact disk (CD) – an early, but still used, optical medium.

Digital versatile disk (DVD) – a later, higher capacity optical medium.

Blu-ray disk – a modern, extremely high capacity optical medium.

DVD devices use a higher frequency laser than CD devices. The higher frequency allows the pits and land to be packed tighter onto the tracks. This allows more data to be stored.

117

Blu-ray devices use a blue-violet laser that operates at a shorter wavelength than the red lasers used in CD and DVD devices. This gives more precision when writing to and reading from a disk. This mean that data can be packed even closer together than when using a DVD device. DVDs and Blu-ray disks can have more than one reflective layer on which data can be stored.

Each type of optical disk has a different storage capacity for data, as shown in Table 8.04.

Table 8.04

Optical disk type	Capacity
CD	700 MB – equivalent of 80 mins of music
DVD single layer	4.7 GB – equivalent of 1.5 hr of standard-definition video and sound
DVD dual layer	9.4 GB – equivalent of 3 hr of standard-definition video and sound
Blu-ray single layer	25 GB – equivalent of 2.5 hr of high-definition video and sound
Blu-ray dual layer	50 GB – equivalent of 5 hr of high-definition video and sound
Blu-ray triple layer	100 GB – equivalent of 10 hr of high-definition video and sound
Blu-ray quadruple layer	128 GB – equivalent of 13 hr of high-definition video and sound

Optical media come in different types:

- ROM – read only. The data stored is already burned onto the disk by a manufacturer or another user. This data can only be read.

- -R. The disk is initially empty of data. It can be written to once and once only. Once written, the data can be read. There is a similar format called +R.

- -RW. The disk is initially empty of data. It can be written to and read from repeatedly. This type of disk has a reflective surface that can have pits burned in to it. By using a higher power laser the surface can be made to flow and cover the pits. This will return the disk to a blank state. There is a similar format called +RW.

Data stored on an optical medium is more portable than that on a hard disk drive. This is because the disk can easily be carried from one location to another. However, optical disks tend to have slower data transfer rates than hard disks and a far lower storage capacity. Most desktop PCs and laptops have a built-in optical disk drive, usually one that is able to burn media as well as read from it. Smaller computers, such as tablets and smartphones, tend to not have an optical disk drive as they are unable to accommodate the physical size of them.

Solid-state storage

Unlike magnetic and optical devices, solid-state storage has no moving parts. Instead, high-speed flash memory is used to store data. Examples of solid-state storage include USB **RAM sticks**, **solid-state hard drives** and **SD cards**.

 KEY TERM

RAM stick – small solid-state medium used to transport data.

Solid-state drive (SSD) – a solid-state equivalent of a hard disk drive.

SD card – a solid-state card used to store and transfer data.

Solid-state devices are physically quite small in size, but their data transfer rate is much quicker than other types of storage. They are capable of rates up to 230 megabytes per second. They are normally no larger than 4 terabytes in capacity. This is because flash memory is expensive to produce.

A solid-state storage device can be written to and read from many times. This, combined with their physically small size, makes them useful as portable storage device. Many portable devices such as tablets and smartphones make use of solid-state storage. They are also used in compact media players, cameras and computers such as the Raspberry Pi.

Off-line storage

Off-line storage is any non-volatile storage device or medium that can be disconnected (off-line), or removed, from a computer. Typical examples of off-line storage include optical media (CD, DVD and Blu-ray disks), USB RAM sticks, external hard drives and magnetic tape.

SYLLABUS CHECK

Provide examples of off-line storage, such as: Digital Versatile Disk (DVD), Compact Disk (CD), Blu-ray disk, USB flash memory and removable HDD.

Describe the principles of operation of a range of storage devices and media including magnetic, optical and solid-state.

TEST YOURSELF

Why might off-line storage be necessary for a business?

8.02 Choosing an appropriate secondary storage device

There are many different types of secondary storage medium. Some types are more suitable for certain situations than others. Selecting the wrong format can have consequences.

SYLLABUS CHECK

Describe how the principles of operation are applied to currently available storage solutions, such as SSDs, HDDs, USB flash memory, DVDs, CDs and Blu-ray disks.

There are several factors to take into account when choosing an appropriate secondary storage medium:

- Capacity – The amount of data that can be stored with the medium.

- Transfer speed – The rate at which data can be transferred to and from the medium.

- Portability – How easily the medium can be transported from one location to another

- Durability – How resistant the medium is to data loss and damage from wear, tear and pressure.

- Cost – How expensive is the medium (this is often calculated as cost per megabyte or cost per gigabyte).

Table 8.05 gives a general comparison of differing media.

Table 8.05

Format/ Device	Capacity	Transfer speed	Portable	Durability	Cost per megabyte
Magnetic					
Hard disk drive	Up to 8 TB	Fast, up to 128 MB per second	Often fixed within a computer Portable versions exist	Very durable	Very cheap
Magnetic tape	Up to 185 TB	Medium, up to 30 MB per second	Yes	Case is quite durable, although tape can be easily damaged	Extremely cheap
Optical					
CD	700 MB	Slow, up to 10 MB per second	Yes	Reflective surface is quite easily scratched Disk is easily broken	Cheap for small volumes, expensive for large data storage
DVD	4.7–9.4 GB	Medium, up to 33 MB per second	Yes	Reflective surface is quite easily scratched Disk is easily broken	Cheap for small volumes, expensive for large data storage
Blu-ray	25–128 GB	Quite quick, up to 72 MB per second	Yes	Reflective surface is quite easily scratched Disk is easily broken	Cheap for small volumes, expensive for large data storage
Solid-state					
USB RAM stick	Up to 1 TB	Very quick, up to 180 MB per second	Yes	Fairly durable, but easily lost	Very cheap
Solid-state drive	Up to 4 TB	Extremely quick, up to 230 MB per second	Yes	Very durable as no moving parts	Expensive
SD card	Up to 2 TB	Medium, up to 48 MB per second	Yes	Fairly durable, but easily lost	Very cheap

Since different secondary storage media have different capabilities, some types are better suited to certain situations than others. Table 8.06 give some uses of the different media.

Table 8.06

Situation	Secondary storage medium	Reasons
Storing operating system, data and programs	Hard disk drive Solid-state drive	• Large capacity • High data transfer rate • Data can be read and written
Distribution of software	CD-ROM DVD-ROM	• Cheap • Easily duplicated • Portable • Once written data cannot be erased or changed
Distribution of films	DVD-ROM Blu-ray ROM	• Larger capacity to deal with large file size of films • Easily duplicated • Portable • Once written data cannot be erased or changed

Situation	Secondary storage medium	Reasons
Transferring data from one computer to another	USB RAM stick SD card	• Cheap • Very portable
Backing up data	Magnetic tape Portable hard disk drive	• Large capacity • Easy to remove and store elsewhere for safe keeping • Data can be over-written to make a new back-up
Archiving data	CD-R DVD-R Blu-ray R	• Easy to remove and store elsewhere for safe keeping • Once written, data cannot be erased or changed

TEST YOURSELF

1 What kind of secondary storage devices do you mostly use?

2 Do you think they are the best choice?

3 Would another type of secondary storage be more suitable?

8.03 Calculating the storage requirement of a file

SYLLABUS CHECK

Calculate the storage requirement of a file.

Data is represented as bits. Data is stored in files and file sizes are represented in units:

$$8 \text{ bits} = 1 \text{ byte, or } 1\,B$$
$$1024 \text{ bytes} = 1 \text{ kilobyte } (1\,KB)$$
$$1024 \text{ kilobytes} = 1 \text{ megabyte } (1\,MB) \text{ or } 1\,048\,576 \text{ bytes}$$
$$1024 \text{ megabytes} = 1 \text{ gigabyte } (1\,GB) \text{ or } 1\,073\,741\,824 \text{ bytes}$$
$$1024 \text{ gigabytes} = 1 \text{ terabyte } (1\,TB) \text{ or } 1\,099\,511\,627\,776 \text{ bytes}$$

The number of bits required for data storage depends on the amount of data and the type of data to be stored.

Table 8.07

Data to be stored	Storage requirements
Pixels in a black and white image	1 bit per pixel
Pixels in an 8-bit colour image	8 bits (1 byte) per pixel
Characters in an ASCII text string	1 byte per character
Sound in a wave file	86 kilobytes per second
Uncompressed frame of standard-definition TV	27 megabytes per frame
Uncompressed frame of high-definition TV	182 megabytes per frame

Compression can be used to reduce file storage requirements.

To learn more about data representation and compression, see Chapter 1.

To calculate the storage requirements of a file we need to know the type and amount of data to be stored.

Example 1: Storing a string of text

The following message is stored in a file:

I LOVE IGCSE COMPUTER SCIENCE!

This message contains 30 characters (including spaces). Each character requires 1 byte for storage. Therefore, the size of the file for this data would be:

30 characters × 1 byte per character = **30 bytes**

Example 2: Storing a simple black-and-white image

The graphic in Figure 8.04 is stored in a file.

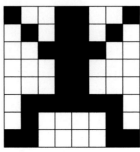

Figure 8.04 Stored simple black-and-white image

The graphic contains 8 rows and 8 columns giving 64 pixels in total: 8 × 8 = 64.

A black and white image requires 1 bit per pixel. Therefore, excluding metadata, the size of the file for this data would be:

64 pixels × 1 bit per pixel = **64 bits or 8 bytes**

Example 3: Storing a simple 8-bit colour image

The 8-bit colour graphic in Figure 8.05 is to be stored in a file.

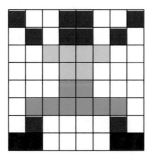

Figure 8.05 Stored 8-bit colour image

The graphic contains 8 rows and 8 columns giving 64 pixels in total. However, this graphic is in 8-bit colour (unlike the black-and-white image of Example 2). This requires 8 bits (1 byte) per pixel. Therefore, excluding metadata, the size of the file for this data would be:

64 pixels × 8 bits = 512 bits
512 bits ÷ 8 = **64 bytes**

Example 4: Calculating a file size from image size and resolution

The file size of an image can be calculated as long as its size and resolution are known. For example, consider a 24-bit colour image that is 2 inches high and 3 inches wide, with a resolution of 300 dots per inch.

First, the number of pixels are calculated. If the resolution is 300 dots per inch then the pixel grid for a 2-inch by 3-inch image will measure 600 pixels (2 × 300) by 900 pixels (3 × 300). As a 24-bit colour image requires 24 bits for each pixel, excluding metadata the size of the file would be:

$$300 \text{ pixels} \times 900 \text{ pixels} = 270\,000 \text{ pixels}$$
$$270\,000 \text{ pixels} \times 24 \text{ bits per pixel} = 6\,480\,000 \text{ bits}$$
$$6\,480\,000 \text{ bits} \div 8 = 810\,000 \text{ bytes}$$
$$810\,000 \text{ bytes} \div 1024 = \mathbf{791.02 \text{ kilobytes}}$$
$$792.02 \div 1024 = \mathbf{0.77 \text{ megabytes}}$$

Example 5: Storing a database

A university holds student data in a simple flat file database with the structure shown in Table 8.08.

Table 8.08

Field Name	Type	Field size	Sample record
StudentID	Number	4	1509
FamilyName	Text	30	Scott
Firstname	Text	20	Heather
Address	Text	30	34 Brampton Rd
Town	Text	20	Swindon
Postcode	Text	8	SN5 5DS
Gender	Text	6	Female
Date of birth	Date	6	01/03/98
Course Name	Text	20	Computer Art

The university's database currently holds data for 27 000 students. In this example, we can only estimate the size of the data. This is because we don't know exactly what data each record has, only what the field size in database structure will allow. The database has nine fields and each record should allow for a total of 144 bytes

$$(4 + 30 + 20 + 30 + 20 + 8 + 6 + 6 + 20).$$

Each data character requires 1 byte for storage. Therefore, the estimated size of the file for this data would be:

$$144 \text{ characters per record} \times 1 \text{ byte per character} = 144 \text{ bytes}$$
$$144 \text{ bytes} \times 27\,000 \text{ records} = 3\,888\,000 \text{ bytes}$$
$$3\,888\,000 \div 1024 = 3796.875 \text{ kilobytes}$$
$$3796.875 \div 1024 = \mathbf{3.71 \text{ megabytes}}$$

Example 6: Calculating the size of an audio file

There are four main pieces of data that are used in calculating the size of an audio file:

- The length of the audio track (this needs to be in seconds)
- The number of samples taken per second (sample rate)
- The number of bits used to store each sample (sample depth)
- The number of channels used to play the track (mono has 1, stereo has 2)

The following calculation can then be carried out to find the size of the file:

sample rate x sample depth × track length × number of tracks

If an audio track is 3 minutes and 30 seconds (210 seconds in total) in length, recorded in stereo, samples at 44 Khz (44000 Hz) with a sample depth of 16 bits, this is how we would calculate the file size:

$$44000 \times 16 \times 210 \times 2 = 295680000 \text{ bits}$$
$$295680000 \div 8 = 36960000 \text{ bytes}$$
$$36960000 \div 1024 = 36093.75 \text{ kilobytes}$$
$$36093.75 \div 1024 = \textbf{35.25 megabytes}$$

Summary

- Data is held in storage for processing and so that it can be retrieved for later use.
- There are three types of storage, primary storage, secondary storage and off-line storage.
- Primary storage is storage internal to the computer that is directly accessible by the processor.
- Random Access Memory (RAM) is primary storage that temporarily holds running programs and data for processing. It is volatile, meaning it loses its contents when switched off.
- Read Only Memory (ROM) is primary storage that can be read from but not written to. ROM is non-volatile, meaning it keeps its contents when power is switched off.
- Secondary storage is non-volatile storage that is not directly accessible by the processor that is used to hold data permanently, till deleted:
  - Magnetic storage uses electromagnets and magnetic fields to read, write and erase data. Magnetic devices are either tape based or disk based.
  - Optical devices shine a laser beam onto a disk with a reflective surface. Data is stored on the disk in the form of indentations (pits) and raised areas (land). Optical devices generally have less capacity and slower data transfer rates than magnetic devices.
  - Solid-state devices have no moving parts. They use high-speed flash memory to store data. SSDs are very fast at transferring data, but generally smaller in capacity and far more expensive than equivalent hard disk drives.
- Off-line storage is any non-volatile storage device or medium that is disconnected (off-line), or removed, from the computer.
- A user must take into account several factors when choosing an appropriate medium such as capacity, data transfer rate, portability, durability and cost per megabyte.
- When calculating the storage requirements for data, the user must take into account the type of data and the amount of data to be stored.

Exam-style questions

1   Explain the difference between primary storage and secondary storage.   (2 marks)

2   Describe three ways in which RAM differs from ROM.   (3 marks)

3   Explain how a hard disk drive reads and writes data.   (4 marks)

4   What enables a Blu-ray disk to hold more data than a compact disk?   (2 marks)

5   A company sends out an electronic catalogue its customers. Suggest a suitable storage medium and justify your choice with reasons.   (2 marks)

6   A 16-bit colour image is 4 inches × 1 inch in size, with a resolution of 600 dots per inch. Calculate the storage requirements for this image.   (1 mark)

7   Explain why data on a magnetic tape may be accessed quickly or slowly.   (2 marks)

8   Explain two reasons why solid-state storage is not as common in desktop PCs and laptops as hard disk drives.   (2 marks)

Chapter 9:
Security

Learning objectives

By the end of this chapter you will:

- understand that data needs to be kept safe from accidental damage
- understand that data needs to be kept safe from malicious actions
- understand how to keep data safe when storing and transmitting, including use of passwords, firewalls, security protocols and symmetric encryption
- understand that online systems need to be kept safe from attacks.

9.01 Introduction

Computer systems are used to store and process data in many ways:

- Companies need to keep data about their customers' accounts.
- Doctors need to keep data about their patients.
- Research scientists need to keep data from experiments.
- Students need to keep data in the form of notes.
- Police need to keep data about their investigations and suspects.

Data has a value. The more accurate and complete the data, the more valuable it is. If data is lost, corrupted or accidentally changed, it loses value. For example, a doctor is less likely to be able to treat an illness correctly if the data held about the patient is not accurate or complete. Therefore it is extremely important to keep data accurate, complete and safe.

It is possible for data to be accidentally, or intentionally, changed or deleted. **Computer security** helps to keep data safe from loss, deletion, change and corruption. This helps maintain the value of the data.

KEY TERM

Computer security – the protection of computers from unauthorised access and the protection of data from loss.

126

Figure 9.01 Computer security

9.02 Security and prevention against accidental data loss or change

SYLLABUS CHECK

Understand the need to keep data safe from accidental damage, including corruption and human errors.

It does not matter how well a computer system is looked after, sometimes data can be damaged unintentionally. Data can be lost, deleted, changed or corrupted in a variety of ways:

- human error – for example, accidental deletion or overwriting of files

- theft – for example, having a laptop or smartphone stolen

- physical causes – for example, fire or water damage to equipment

- power failure – resulting in data in volatile memory (RAM) not being saved to permanent memory

- hardware failure – for example, a damaged hard disk drive

- misplacing portable media – for example, DVDs and memory sticks.

TEST YOURSELF

If a personal laptop was stolen, what personal or sensitive data might fall into someone else's hands?

Two methods of computer security can be implemented to help prevent unintentional loss of data:

- Backups of data help to retrieve data when it is lost.

- Verification helps to prevent data loss occurring.

Backups

Data can be accidentally lost. A laptop could be stolen or a computer hard disk drive could fail. Once data is lost we cannot get it back. A sensible safety measure is to make a copy of the data. A backup is a copy of data being used that we can keep in case of data loss. The data is copied onto a separate storage medium and this is kept separate from the main system. If we accidentally lose, corrupt or delete our data, the copy of the data can be transferred back to the computer system.

We can back up data onto various storage media:

- magnetic media – for example, external hard disk drives and magnetic tape

- optical media – for example, CDs, DVDs and Blu-ray disks

- cloud storage – for example, smartphone manufacturers provide online backup facilities so that phone data can be automatically backed up each day.

To learn more about backup storage media, see Chapter 8.

In order for a backup to be of any value we must update it regularly. How frequently a backup needs to be made depends on the situation:

- A bank might make backups several times each day because of the number of financial transactions taking place and the importance they have.

- A doctor's surgery may make a backup of patient records each evening.

- A school might make a backup of student and teacher records at the end of each week.

- A home user might make a backup occasionally.

Additionally, backups can be made automatically or manually. Most organisations employ automatic backups, where the computer system automatically makes a copy of the data. Home users frequently make manual backups, as and when they remember to, or feel the need to do so.

Verification

As we are human we can make mistakes. It can be quite easy for us to accidentally overwrite, change or delete a file. Although backups can help to retrieve lost data, it is also sensible to try and prevent data loss from occurring in the first place. To help guard against data loss many computer systems use a method known as verification.

Verification is a check that asks the user to confirm whether or not they wish to go ahead with an instruction. The confirmation usually takes the form of a question in a dialogue box, to which the user responds with a confirmation or cancellation. For example, computer systems usually ask for verification in the following situations:

- when attempting to save a file with a filename that already exists in that location
- when copying an older version of a file into a folder that contains a newer version of that document
- when deleting a record or amending data in a database.

Verification forces the user to stop and think about the action they intend to perform. However, verification is not foolproof. Users may still confirm an action, such as deleting a file, without realising the consequences until later.

Figure 9.02 Verification message

9.03 Unauthorised access to computer systems and data

As well as trying to avoid accidental loss of data, it also needs to be kept safe from unauthorised access. Data may be sensitive and private for example, patient data or a person's financial data. Preventing unauthorised users from accessing data is just as, if not more, important than protecting the data's value.

Data on a computer system can be accessed locally or online. With local access, the user has physical access to the computer system and its data. With online access, the user is able to access the computer system and its data via a network or the internet.

Unauthorised attempts at accessing data are known as 'attacks'. Attacks can come in several different ways:

- malware

- phishing

- pharming

- denial of service (DoS) attacks.

Malware

Some attacks come in the form of software called 'malware'. Malware is designed to disrupt or modify a computer system and its data. Malware is installed on a computer system without the user's knowledge. The software is accidentally downloaded from email attachments, USB RAM sticks and websites. Once installed, malware can cause considerable damage, or at the least, great inconvenience.

There are different types of malware:

- Viruses are self-replicating software that are designed to disrupt the normal operation of a computer. They can cause data loss by deleting and corrupting files.

- Worms are programs that do not delete or corrupt files. Instead they replicate themselves over and over, filling a computer's storage. This can cause a computer to run slowly or stop running altogether.

- Trojan horses are programs that disguise themselves as other programs. When run, they act like any other virus, deleting and corrupting files.

- Spyware are programs that collect personal and sensitive data, then send it to the spyware's authors.

Figure 9.03 Internet risks

To learn more about malware see Chapter 2.

Phishing

One way of gaining access to data is simply to ask for it. This is the basis of phishing. Phishing was given its name because it is, like fishing, an attempt to gain something (in this case data) by using bait. A phishing attack usually comes in the form of an email. The email will look like it is from a person or organisation that is known to and trusted by the user. For example, many phishing emails look like they come from banks or online auction sites. The email often states that there is a problem with the user's online account and asks for confirmation of personal data to investigate the issue. It is designed to trick a user into giving data such as bank account details, or usernames and passwords to websites.

A phishing email normally looks like a genuine email, but usually asks the user to click on a hyperlink. The hyperlink transfers the user to a fake website that looks like the organisation's real website. The website then asks the user to enter their personal data. Once given, the data is used by criminals to steal money or buy items online.

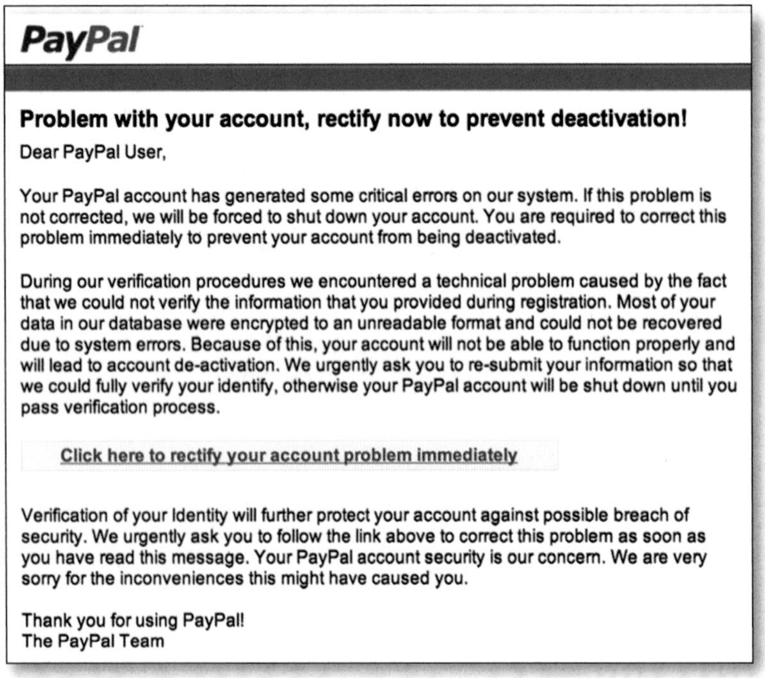

PayPal

Problem with your account, rectify now to prevent deactivation!

Dear PayPal User,

Your PayPal account has generated some critical errors on our system. If this problem is not corrected, we will be forced to shut down your account. You are required to correct this problem immediately to prevent your account from being deactivated.

During our verification procedures we encountered a technical problem caused by the fact that we could not verify the information that you provided during registration. Most of your data in our database were encrypted to an unreadable format and could not be recovered due to system errors. Because of this, your account will not be able to function properly and will lead to account de-activation. We urgently ask you to re-submit your information so that we could fully verify your identify, otherwise your PayPal account will be shut down until you pass verification process.

<u>Click here to rectify your account problem immediately</u>

Verification of your Identity will further protect your account against possible breach of security. We urgently ask you to follow the link above to correct this problem as soon as you have read this message. Your PayPal account security is our concern. We are very sorry for the inconveniences this might have caused you.

Thank you for using PayPal!
The PayPal Team

Figure 9.04 Phishing email

Pharming

Phishing uses emails to help capture data by tricking a user into visiting a fake website. Pharming also attempts to trick the user into giving their personal data by using fake websites. When a user tries to visit a genuine website, they are instead re-directed to a fake website that looks very much like the real site. Once the user enters their personal data, such as their user ID and password, the data is passed to criminals.

Pharming can happen because of the way the internet works. Each website has a domain name that is translated into an IP address. The user's browser is directed to the IP address, giving access to the website. With pharming, malware installed on the user's computer looks for domain names of reputable sites and translates them into different IP addresses, those of fake websites. Instead of visiting a genuine website, the user is directed to the fake website instead.

To learn more about IP addresses and how the internet works, see Chapter 2.

Denial of Service (DoS) attacks

Denial of Service (DoS) attacks take their name from their purpose: to deny a service. DoS attacks are not designed to gain access to data. Instead they prevent access to data.

Websites and networks are accessed through **servers**. When a user's computer wants to access data on a server, it sends a transmission known as a **request**. The server acknowledges the request and sends the requested data to the user.

KEY TERM

Server – a computer which handles requests from other computers.

Request – a communication which asks for data to be transferred.

There are only so many requests that a server handle at any one time. The more powerful the server, the more requests it can handle. When a large number of requests are received, each request is placed into a queue and dealt with in turn. A DoS attack attempts to prevent access to a server by sending it more requests than it can handle. The request queue becomes so large that the server cannot respond to all requests within a reasonable time, preventing it from providing a service.

DoS attacks are usually attacks that come from one computer. Another form of DoS attack is where two or more computers attack a server at the same time. This is known as a Distributed Denial of Service (DDoS) attack because the requests are distributed among a number of computers. Usually, the attacking computers are infected with malware that instructs the computer to continually send requests to a server.

TEST YOURSELF

Hundreds of DoS attacks occur every day. Use the Internet to find out about two high-profile organisations whose websites have been subject to DoS attacks and research why they were targeted.

9.04 Security and protection against attacks

SYLLABUS CHECK

Understand how data are kept safe when stored and transmitted, including:

- use of passwords, both entered at a keyboard and biometric
- use of firewalls, both software and hardware, including proxy servers
- use of security protocols such as Secure Socket Layer (SSL) and Transport Layer Security (TLS)
- use of symmetric encryption (plain text, cypher text and the use of a key) showing understanding that increasing the length of a key increases the strength of the encryption.

Be able to describe how the knowledge discussed in this chapter can be applied to real-life scenarios including, for example, online banking and shopping.

There are several ways in which computer security can be implemented to keep data safe from unauthorised access, alteration and deletion:

- physical security
- authentication
- anti-virus software
- firewalls.

- proxy servers
- protocols
- encryption

Each method helps to prevent different forms of unauthorised access to data.

Physical security

KEY TERM

Physical security – security which prevents physical access to a computer.

Our data is often of a sensitive or private nature. We need to keep our data safe from users who do not have the authority, or permission, to access it.

Physical security prevents local access to the system and data. This security can be implemented in several ways:

- Locks – The computer system and data can be kept in a locked room. Organisations that hold sensitive and private data keep their computer systems, data and backups locked away. This way only authorised users can have physical access.

- CCTV – Cameras can be used to monitor who physically accesses a system. CCTV can help deter users who have no authority as they know they will be seen accessing the data.

- Security guards – Where data is especially sensitive, security guards are often employed as an extra level of security to help deter those users who do not have permission to access a computer system.

Physical security methods are simple to implement and can be quite effective. However, all they do is prevent or deter a user from accessing data without permission. Physical methods cannot help recover data that has been lost.

Figure 9.05 CCTV can be used to deter an unauthorised user from attempting to access a system

Authentication

A user can gain access a computer system and its data either locally or remotely. Physical security attempts to prevent physical access, but once physical access is gained another form of prevention is necessary. **Authentication** is designed to stop a user from being able to access the system once they have physically got to it. Additionally, it guards against an unauthorised user attempting to gain access remotely, for example over the internet.

KEY TERM

Authentication – security which prevents access to a computer even if the user has physical access.

In modern computer systems the most common form of authentication used is the combination of user identification (user ID) and password protection. A user ID is the name a user uses to identify themselves to a computer system. User IDs often take the form of the user's name. A password is a secret word or series of characters, known only by the user, that pairs with the user ID. Only the correct combination of user ID and password allows access to the system. For example, John Smith may use the string 'computingisfun' as the password for the user ID 'johnsmith'. Table 9.01 shows what happens when he enters certain values.

Table 9.01

User ID	Password	Result
John_smith	computing	Incorrect match. Access denied
johnsmith	computingisfun	Correct match. Access granted

A user ID and password can be a fairly secure method of preventing unauthorised access to a computer system and its data. However, some users can make it quite easy for someone else to guess their password by choosing a password that is data associated with them, such as:

- their date of birth
- the name of a daughter, son, brother, sister or other family member
- the name of their pet
- their initials
- a favourite item, hobby or place.

A password of this nature is often referred to as a 'weak' password. This is because it can be easily determined. A strong password is one that is very difficult for someone else to guess. A password is considered to be strong if it:

- is at least eight characters in length
- does not contain your user ID, real name, or organisation name
- does not contain a complete word
- is significantly different from previous passwords
- uses a mixture of characters from the keyboard, including upper and lower case letters, numbers and symbols.

Nancy Bauer enjoys computing. She has a pet called Felix. Her user ID is nancybauer. Passwords she might choose could include:

Table 9.02

User ID	Password	Strength
nancybauer	nancy	Weak – too few characters and features her name
nancybauer	felix	Weak – too few characters and is the name of her pet
nancybauer	F3l1x	Medium – too short, but uses a combination of letters and numbers
nancybauer	$0cC3ri5fuN	Strong – more than 8 characters, more than one word, a mixture of uppercase and lowercase letters, numbers and symbols

TEST YOURSELF

1   Think of a password you use regularly. How strong is it? How could you make it stronger?
2   Why is it important to have both physical security and authentication when creating a secure system?

Another problem that can occur is that users often use the same passwords for different systems. It is sensible for us to use different passwords for each system we have access to.

Passwords were first used with computers in the 1960s. Since then they have become the most commonly used form of authentication. Amongst other things, passwords are now used to:

- log on to a PC or network

- confirm banking transactions

- gain access to a wireless network

- log onto online services

- access emails.

Passwords are widely used but they can be easy to guess. As a result, security experts have looked for alternative methods of preventing unauthorised access to systems and data.

Biometrics

Humans have individual physical characteristics: fingerprints, voice patterns, face shapes and iris patterns.

As physical characteristics are unique, they provide a unique way to identify a user to a computer system. The use of physical characteristics as a means of identification is known as 'biometrics'. Several biometric systems have been introduced as alternative means of authentication. Unlike passwords that are typed in using a keyboard, biometrics use scanners or sensors to record input.

Fingerprint scanners require a user to place their finger against a scanner and an image of their fingerprint is taken. The computer compares the series of ridges and bumps recorded in the image with a fingerprint image previously taken. The user is only granted access if they match. Fingerprint scanners are fairly cheap to implement and are regarded as a reasonably reliable means of authentication. However, fingerprint authentication is unsuitable for children as a child's fingerprint pattern alters as they grow.

Figure 9.06 A finger print scanner

Voice recognition software requires the user to speak a phrase known to the computer into a microphone. Access is only granted to the system if the phrase and voice pattern match those stored by the computer. Voice recognition is a fairly reliable technology but it suffers in noisy environments where the computer can have difficulty in hearing the voice amongst the background noise. The recognition may also fail if the user has a cold or a sore throat, as it may alter their voice.

Facial recognition uses a camera to take an image of the user's face. The computer notes the size and shape of facial features, such as eyes, nose and cheekbones, and the distances between them. Access is only granted to the system if the pattern matches that stored by the system for the user. Facial recognition is reasonably reliable, but can fail if poor lighting causes facial features to be incorrectly measured. Additionally, changes in hairstyle, or wearing glasses, can affect reliability.

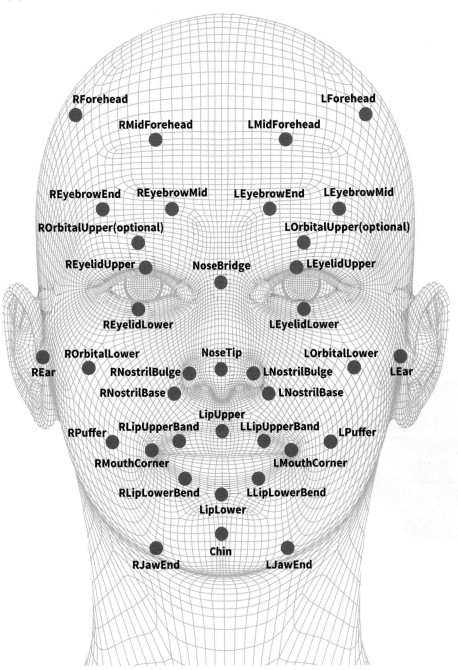

Figure 9.07 Facial recognition software measures many different facial features

Iris scanners require the user to place their eye to a scanner. This records a high resolution and detailed image of their iris pattern. Access is only granted if the image pattern matches that stored by the system. Iris recognition is highly reliable but expensive to implement. Some users can find having their eye scanned an uncomfortable experience.

Figure 9.08 An iris being scanned

Biometric technology is improving but it is still regarded as far from perfect. As a result, many systems include an alternative method of authentication for situations where biometric authentication fails.

TEST YOURSELF

Think of potential problems that a disabled user might face when using biometric authentication?

Anti-virus software

It can be extremely difficult to detect and remove malware once it is installed on a computer. Special software known as **anti-virus software** is needed to find and delete malware.

KEY TERM

Anti-virus software – software which finds and remove viruses from a computer by scanning it.

Anti-virus software uses a list of known malware ('virus definitions') and how they work. The software scans the computer and looks for any malware that it can recognise. If it finds any malware, the anti-virus software attempts to remove it or block its access to the computer.

Anti-virus software can only detect infection from known viruses. New viruses are released all the time. In order to remain effective, anti-virus software needs to have up-to-date virus definitions.

To learn more about anti-virus software see Chapter 2.

Firewalls

Computers communicate and transfer data by sending messages. Messages that are sent and received by computers are known as 'traffic'. Although most of the traffic is of a genuine nature, such as the downloading of an email, other traffic is unauthorised. For example:

- spyware may transmit the personal data it has gathered back to its creator

- DoS malware may continually send requests to a server

- malware may attempt to download other malware

- email viruses might attempt to send spam to other computers.

A firewall is a security technology that monitors incoming and outgoing traffic. It provides a protective barrier between the computer and other computers. Firewalls work through the use of rules. Different rules exist for different types of traffic, for example:

- only certain programs can be allowed to send and receive traffic

- access to certain websites or servers can be blocked.

The traffic is examined by the firewall and checked against the set rules. If it meets the rules the traffic is forwarded, otherwise it is blocked, preventing unauthorised access to and from the computer.

Two types of firewall exist, hardware firewalls and software firewalls. Hardware firewalls protect a network, whereas a software firewall protects an individual computer. Many routers contain hardware firewalls that monitor traffic between a network and the internet. Software firewalls have to be installed on each computer on a network.

Firewalls are very effective at blocking unauthorised access. However, because users can modify the rules, unauthorised traffic may still occur.

Proxy servers

One way to protect a server from attacks is to prevent direct access to the server itself. This is done by directing traffic to an intermediary server. This is known as a proxy server. The proxy server sits between the main server and the internet.

The purpose of the proxy server is to direct traffic away from the network server. When a request comes in from the internet, the proxy server examines the request. If the request is thought to be valid, the corresponding data is retrieved from the network server and transmitted to the requesting computer. As a result, any attack hits only the proxy server, not the network server itself.

Proxy servers can also contain copies of data. This brings several benefits:

- If the data on a proxy server is lost, corrupted or changed (accidentally or maliciously) the original data is still safe and secure on the network server.

- A proxy server may hold certain data, but not other, more sensitive data. An external computer can only access the data on the proxy server, not the sensitive data held on the network server.

- As a proxy server can handle requests and transfer data, the network server is free to handle requests from computers on its own network, speeding up internal access times.

- A proxy server can hold copies of frequently visited webpages. This speeds up access to those pages from computers on the network as the pages do not have to be downloaded from the internet.

- A proxy server can be used to prevent users on a network from accessing external websites. Many schools use this system to prevent students from accessing unsuitable material.

- An organisation that receives large amounts of requests can use several proxy servers to help spread the load. Popular websites use this method to speed up response times.

Encryption

It does not matter how much protection a computer system has, the data it contains may still end up in the hands of an unauthorised user. Another method to protect the data is to convert it into a form that cannot be understood by anyone other than an authorised user. This process is called **encryption**. Encryption does not prevent data from being accessed. It prevents the data being understood by unauthorised user if it is accessed.

 KEY TERM

Encryption – a way of modifying data to make it difficult to understand if intercepted.

Key – information that describes how a message is encrypted or decrypted.

Encryption works by using a **key**. A key is a particular piece of information that is required to disguise (encrypt) and reveal (decrypt) the data.

One of the earliest known methods of encryption is the Caesar cipher, named after Julius Caesar who is said to have used it to disguise private messages. The Caesar cipher works by taking each letter in the alphabet and replacing it with another letter several positions up or down the alphabet. The number of positions is called the offset. In this encryption method, the offset is the key.

For example, a cipher with an offset of 4 would replace each letter with that four places above in the alphabet. 'A' would become 'E', 'B' would become 'F' and so on as shown in Table 9.03.

Table 9.03

Plaintext	A	B	C	D	E	F	G	H	I	J	K	L	M	N	O	P	Q	R	S	T	U	V	W	X	Y	Z
Offset = 4	E	F	G	H	I	J	K	L	M	N	O	P	Q	R	S	T	U	V	W	X	Y	Z	A	B	C	D

To encrypt a message, each letter in the message is replaced with its offset equivalent. For example:

I LOVE COMPUTER SCIENCE

becomes

M PSZI GSQTYXIV WGMIRGI

To decrypt a message, the process is reversed.

This cipher is extremely simple to break, as there are only 25 possible keys that can be used. Modern encryptions use extremely complex algorithms and keys to encrypt data.

There are various encryption algorithms available and all of them use keys. An encrypted message can be decrypted by anyone who knows the encryption method and the encryption key. To make it more difficult for an unauthorised user to decrypt a message, a long key must be used.

Keys are created from numbers generated using binary digits. The number of binary digits used is known as the key length. The longer the key length, the more possible combinations there are to generate numbers.

Table 9.04

Size of key in bits	Number of possible combinations
1	2
2	4
8	256
16	65 536
32	4 294 967 296
128	More than 300 000 000 000 000 000 000 000 000 000 000

Computers are used to generate keys, they can also be used to try and determine what key has been used. They do this by generating every possible number combination in a key length and trying it to decrypt the message. This is known as a brute force attack. Modern encryption methods use 128-bit keys. This gives a range of combinations so big that even supercomputers cannot generate every possible combination.

Encryption can be symmetric or asymmetric. In symmetric encryption (such as the Caesar cipher), the same key is used to encrypt and decrypt the message. This means that two people with the key can share messages. The problem with this method is that anyone who obtains the key can encrypt or decrypt a message. Messages sent over networks, or over the internet, can be intercepted. Therefore if the key is known by unauthorised users the encryption is useless.

This fault can be overcome by using asymmetric encryption. Asymmetric encryption uses two keys that work as a pair. The first key is used to encrypt the message. A message encrypted with the first key cannot be decrypted with that same key. It can only be decrypted with the second key. Similarly, a message encrypted with the second key can only be decrypted with the first key.

The first key can be sent to anyone from whom the user wants to receive an encrypted message. As a result, this key is called a 'public key'. The second key is kept secret by the user, so that only they know it. As a result, this key is called a 'private key'. As long as the private key is kept secret, the encryption is extremely difficult to break.

Asymmetric encryption is widely used by organisations who need to send confidential data, for example banks and online shops. When a user logs onto a bank's website, a copy of the bank's public key is downloaded to the user's browser. Any communications sent from the bank to the user are encrypted with the private key. The user's browser decrypts the message using the public key. Similarly, any messages sent from the user's browser are encrypted with the public key. Only the bank, which holds the private key, can decrypt them.

A further advantage of asymmetric encryption is that the source of the message can be trusted. For example, a user connected to an online bank can trust the messages they receive, because only the bank has the key to encrypt the messages.

9.05 Protocols

Different computers communicate in different ways. They are similar to people, who speak different languages. Before computers can communicate with each other they need to agree on how to communicate. They do this by determining and agreeing a set of rules, known as 'protocols'.

Various protocols exist and each one is specific to a purpose:

- Hyper Text Transfer Protocol (HTTP) governs communications across the internet.

- Hyper Text Transfer Protocol Secure (HTTPS) is a more secure version of HTTP, often used to handle financial transactions.

- File Transfer Protocol (FTP) governs the transfer of files across the internet.

- Simple Mail Transfer Protocol (SMTP) handles email communication.

- Transfer Control Protocol/Internet Protocol (TCP/IP) handles communications on a network.

- Voice Over Internet Protocol (VoIP) handles audio/visual communication.

To learn more about protocols, see Chapter 2.

KEY TERM

Secure Socket Layer (SSL) – a protocol which allows secure links between computers.
Transport Layer Security (TLS) – a recent, more secure version of SSL.

HTTPS makes use of another protocol known as **Secure Socket Layer (SSL)**. SSL makes it possible for the internet to be used safely for online transactions and for sensitive data to be safely transmitted. It uses asymmetric encryption to create a secure link between one computer and another. For example, a web server uses SSL to create a link between itself and another computer's web browser. A user can then transfer securely data such as a credit card number or bank account details.

SSL is used to secure:

- online credit card transactions

- any sensitive information exchanged online

- the transfer of files over HTTPS and FTP services such as those sent by website owners updating new pages on their websites

- web-based email

- the connection between an email client and email servers

- cloud-based storage systems

- intranets and extranets

- virtual private networks.

Transport Layer Security (TLS) is a more recent version of SSL. TLS works the same way as SSL, but is more secure as many security issues that arose with SSL were fixed with the development of TLS.

Summary

- Data is valuable. It loses its value if it is lost, accidentally changed or corrupted.

- Computer security is the protection of computer systems and their data.

- Data can be lost accidentally through human error, theft, damage to equipment, power failure, hardware failure or misplacing portable media.

- Backups and verification help protect against accidental data loss. A backup is a copy of data, kept away from the computer system.

- Verification is a check which asks the user to confirm whether or not they wish to go ahead with an action.

- An unauthorised attempt to access a computer is known as an attack. As well as physical attacks (where the user has physical access to the computer), attacks can be made through the use of malware, phishing, pharming and Denial of Service (DoS).

- Malware is software that is designed to affect the normal operation of a computer. Malware comes in the form of viruses, worms, Trojan horses and spyware. Each form of malware can cause data loss or provide unauthorised access to data.

- Phishing is a technique which uses email to trick a user into giving away personal data.

- Pharming directs the user to a fake websites where they may inadvertently give away personal data

- Denial of service attacks attempt to prevent access to data. A computer is used to overload a server with requests.

- Encryption is a technique that disguises the contents of a message using a key.

- Protocols are sets of rules that handle communication between computers.

- Secure Socket Layer (SSL) is a protocol that creates a secure, encrypted link between one computer and another. TLS is an updated, more secure version of SSL.

Exam-style questions

1 What is meant by data losing its value?   (2 marks)

2 Explain what is meant by an automatic backup.   (2 marks)

3 Explain how phishing and pharming trick a user into giving up personal data.   (4 marks)

4 Explain how anti-virus software may help to prevent distributed denial of   (2 marks)
   service attacks.

5 Explain why computer security is more effective when anti-virus software and   (4 marks)
   firewalls are used.

6 Describe how a proxy server can help keep data safe.   (2 marks)

7 Explain the difference between symmetric and asymmetric encryption.   (4 marks)

8 Describe what a protocol is and how protocols help protect data.   (2 marks)

Chapter 10:
Ethics

Learning objectives

By the end of this chapter you will:

- understand the importance of computer ethics
- understand the difference between free software, freeware and shareware
- understand the ethical issues involved in electronic communication.

10.01 Computer ethics

SYLLABUS CHECK

Show understanding of computer ethics, including copyright issues and plagiarism.

There are a number of issues that can arise through the use of computers. This can be through the creation and design of them to using, or misusing, them to communicate. In order to regulate the use of computers a number of **ethics** were developed. These ethics govern and regulate the use of computers, providing laws and guidelines for computer use.

KEY TERM

Ethics – guidelines that state whether something is right or wrong.

Govern – to influence or provide legal authority on a product or process.

Standards – a level of conduct or morals that should be met.

We use the term 'ethical' to mean if something is right or wrong. However, what one person thinks is right, another may think is wrong. Therefore, not everyone agrees on a set of ethics. For example, would it be ethical for a government to store a database of the DNA of everyone in its population, so that when a crime is committed it can immediately check any evidence against the database? How might the population feel about this? What would be the implications?

Computer ethics differ from country to country, as do the laws that **govern** the use of computers. We will cover the general concept of computer ethics and how they are necessary.

Figure 10.01 Wordle of ethics

Technology is constantly developing and people are becoming more reliant upon it in their daily lives. As the world of technology develops, the world of ethics is forced to try to evolve too, creating new ethical **standards** to address new technological advances.

10.02 Copyright and plagiarism

It is very easy to take content from the internet and duplicate it. This could be in a school essay or using an image to promote a product. We can literally just copy the content and insert it into our own document. We could then go on to say that this work is our own work, hoping that no-one would know any different. Would this be ethical? How would you feel if you had displayed your work on the internet, to find that someone else had taken it and said it was their own?

Computer ethics would say that this is wrong to do without the author's permission. Taking the content without the author's permission could be seen as stealing. The author may have taken a lot of time and effort to create the image or content and should be recognised or paid if a person wants to use it. By seeking the owner's permission it gives them the opportunity to ethically allow a person to use their work.

The act of taking another person's work and trying to pass it off as our own is called **plagiarism**. The least we should do if we use the work of another is credit them in our own work. In order to protect their work a person can choose to **copyright** it. A country will usually have a law that governs copyright. This law will have a process that a person needs to go through (usually completing an application) to copyright their work. Once a person's work has a copyright, this gives them the legal right to sole distribution of their work and means they can charge other people money to use it. If another person steals work that has a copyright, this would be breaking the law and there will be set consequences for this. When a person has got a copyright on their work they can display the copyright symbol. This is usually a letter C in a circle.

KEY TERM

Plagiarism – stealing the work of another without making reference to the source where it was obtained.

Copyright – legally protecting work to give the sole right to distribute the work, often with payment.

Figure 10.02 The copyright symbol

Jane Goodall is an author. In early 2013 she wrote a book called *Seeds of Hope: Wisdom and wonder from the world of plants*. The book was about genetically modified crops. When people started reading the book it was famously noticed that much of the text had been taken from well recognised sources such as Wikipedia. The text had been copied without any credit to the original source being made. Further investigation was made into the extent of the plagiarism and it was found that various interviews in the book were also not her own work and had been copied from other sources. Goodall apologised for the plagiarism, but her reputation was damaged as a result.

It is very important to understand who owns our data and information as in some cases uploading it to the World Wide Web may mean that we no longer do own the rights to it. For example, it is written into the terms and conditions of some social networking sites that if we upload images or content, they become the property of the site. This may mean that even if we delete them from the site they can still keep a copy and distribute it if they want to.

TEST YOURSELF

1 Find out what copyright laws exist in your country.
2 Research, using the internet, another famous case of plagiarism.

10.03 Free software, freeware and shareware

SYLLABUS CHECK

Distinguish between free software, freeware and shareware.

One product that people own and copyright is software. We may need to pay for software but in some cases it can be provided free of charge. Software that we can use for free can sometimes have certain conditions placed on its use. We will look at three different types of software that we can use for free.

KEY TERM

Free software – software that we have the freedom to run, share, copy and change.

Freeware – a copy of software given to a person free of charge that cannot be changed or redistributed due to copyright.

Shareware – a free trial or limited version of software.

Free software

Software that is classed as **free software** means that we have the right to run, copy, share and change the software. We can do all this without seeking any permission. The 'free' part of free software is more about the freedom to do whatever you want with the software, it is not in reference to the price paid for the software. A person may still charge or be charged a fee to distribute the software.

Therefore, if a store gives us a free copy of a piece of software, this does not mean that it is classed as free software. This is because we may not have the freedom to share and distribute the software. Unless we do, it is not classed as free software.

Even though we may have the freedom to change and distribute this software, or obtain a copy free of charge, we should not be unethical in how we do this. If we obtained a copy of free software for little or no charge, then distributed the software for a large fee, would this be ethical?

Freeware

Freeware is software that has a copyright but the owner of the software chooses to give away a copy for free. This means that the author does not charge a fee for the software but they still retain the copyright for it. Therefore we cannot do anything other than use the software, we cannot copy it, amend it or share it as we do not own the copyright. If we wanted to do anything with the software other than run it, we would have to ask the owner's permission to do so.

If a software company gave us a free copy of their software that they still retain the copyright for, then we shared this with our friends and family, would this be ethical?

Shareware

Shareware is software that is sometimes distributed or free, but if we like the product the owner will often request a fee. An example of this would be a free trial of a piece of software. Some software companies will distribute a full version of their software as a trial. When the trial time, for example a 30-day period, is up they will require us to pay a fee to continue using the software. Some software companies may give away a version of their software that is limited in features from the full piece of software. To use the full version of the software the company will require us to pay a fee. Both of these, until a version is purchased, are classed as shareware.

> **TEST YOURSELF**
>
> Think of any free software, freeware or shareware that you have used?

10.04 Ethics in electronic communications

> **SYLLABUS CHECK**
>
> Show understanding of the ethical issues raised by the spread of electronic communication and computer systems, including hacking, cracking and production of malware.

When we communicate with others using the internet or other networks, we can put the information we exchange at risk. These risks can include hacking, cracking and malware.

Our data is very precious to us, so we should keep it as safe as possible. For the same reason, we should not try and steal anybody else's data. Doing this would be unethical. Many people will try to obtain our personal data as it can be very valuable. They can use it to sell to marketing companies so they can target us with advertisements. They could also use it to commit identity theft.

> **KEY TERM**
>
> **Hacked** – access gained to a system unlawfully by breaking through security methods.
> **Cracked** – access gained to a system, software or website with the purpose of changing or defacing it.
> **Malware** – a computer program designed to disrupt or damage a computer system.

If we store our personal data on our computer or we provide a company with it and they store it on a computer, if the computer is connected to a network this data could be **hacked**. This means that someone could try to gain unlawful access in order to steal our data. They normally do this through writing a computer program that enables them to gain access. Gaining access in this way would be unethical. The data a hacker may access is not their data and they do not have any ownership rights to it.

A software company could be at risk of their software being **cracked**. When software is cracked a person breaks into the software, disregarding the copyright, and changes the software. They could also crack the software by breaking the need to register the software to use it. A fee may be charged by the software company to use their software, but cracking the software would mean the software could be used without paying this fee. Both changing software that has a copyright and cheating a software company out of their fee is unethical.

A hacker and a cracker are different: a hacker aims to get past a security system, often with the aim to prove they can; a cracker will break into or change a system, website or software with the aim to amend or deface it.

Our computer system can also be affected by **malware**. Malware can be downloaded onto our system in a number of ways. It can often be attached to email communications and is downloaded onto our computer when we open the attachment or click a link. Malware is often used disrupt or damage our computer system. In a strange sense some people believe it is entertaining to create malware programs that will damage other people's computer systems. To create a program and use it for this purpose is unethical. Damaging another person's property for any reason is wrong, especially when it is for their own entertainment.

To learn more about hacking, cracking and malware, see Chapter 2 and Chapter 9.

TEST YOURSELF

If a hacker tries to gain access to a computer system, other than their own, that stores their data, is this unethical?

Summary

- Ethics regulate the use of computers. They provide guidelines and laws for their use.
- Not everyone will agree on a set of ethics as what one person thinks is right, another may think is wrong.
- The act of taking another person's work and trying to pass it off as our own is called 'plagiarism'.
- Copyright allows a person to protect their work. It means that a person must seek the owner's permission in order to use their work.
- Software that is classed as free software means that we have the right to run, copy, share and change the software. We can do all this without seeking any permission.
- Freeware is software that has a copyright but the owner of the software chooses to give away a copy for free.
- An example of shareware is a free trial for software. It is software that is distributed for free at first, but a fee is required for continued use.
- Hacking is gaining unauthorised access to data on a computer, normally with the aim of stealing it.
- Cracking is breaking into a system or software with the aim of changing or defacing it.
- Malware is often used disrupt or damage our computer system. Malware can often be attached to email communications and is downloaded onto our computer when we open the attachment or click a link.

Exam-style questions

1   Define the term 'computer ethics'.   (2 marks)

2   Explain why ethics are necessary when using computers.   (2 marks)

3   If a company gave you a free version of their software and encouraged you to   (1 mark)
    try and improve it and share it with the online community, what kind of software
    would this be?

4   Explain how malware can be distributed using electronic communications.   (2 marks)

5   Explain why it might be unethical to use an image taken from the internet in a   (2 marks)
    commercial website.

Chapter 11:
Programming Concepts

Learning objectives

By the end of this chapter you will:

- understand what variables and constants are and how to use them
- understand what the basic data types are and how to use them
- understand the basic principles of programming, such as sequence, selection, iteration, totalling and counting
- understand what predefined procedures and functions are
- be able to declare and use a one-dimensional array
- understand how to use a variable as an index in an array
- be able to read and write values into an array.

11.01 Introduction

In order to develop your skills as a programmer you need to understand the basic principles and structures involved in programming. The firmer an understanding of these basic principles you have, the better a programmer you are likely to be. So let us develop your understanding!

11.02 Variables and constants

SYLLABUS CHECK

Declare and use variables and constants.

KEY TERM

Variable – a named data location in a program for a value that can be changed.

Constant – a named data location in a program for a value that does not change.

A **variable** is a storage location. It is a named value that contains data that can be changed throughout the execution of a program. A variable will be created and assigned a value at a certain point in a program. This means the variable can then be used repeatedly throughout the program, even changing its value if it is reassigned a new one.

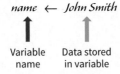

Figure 11.01 Variable information

Variables can be given almost any name, but sensible names should be given that are connected to the data that will be stored in them. It is also good practice to avoid putting spaces in variable names as it can cause some issues.

At the start of a program we could assign the data 'John Smith' to our variable 'name'. However during our program we may assign various other values to the variable, such as 'Alice Jones' or 'Aditya Bhambra'. We keep the name of the variable as 'name': it is the data that is stored in the variable that changes.

A **constant** is also a storage location. It is a named location that contains a value that we don't want to change during the running of the program, e.g. we want the value stored there to remain constant. Constants can be very useful in programming: you only need to change the value where the constant is defined and it will change in every other place it is used within the program. We could have a constant called 'name' that stores the data 'John Smith' and it will store the same data throughout the program.

The difference between a variable and a constant is that the value stored in a variable can be changed throughout a program, but a value stored within a constant will remain the same throughout the program.

11.03 Data types

A variety of data types can be stored in a variable or a constant including strings, integers, real numbers, characters and Boolean data. Normally a variable or a constant will be assigned a suitable data type for the data that it will store.

String

A string is the name given to a series of characters or symbols. We may more commonly call a string 'text'. In some programming languages a variable can be stored as a string by putting quotation marks around the data:

name ← "John Smith"

Sometimes we may need to convert another variable into a string. Programming languages will normally have a built-in method to convert variables between data types.

Numbers

An integer is a whole number that has no decimal points, for example 100 would be an integer but 100.1 would not. Integers are used in programming to store data that would never need to be a decimal or a fraction. For example, a program that stored the year that a person was born would use an integer for this. A year, such as 2001, will never be a decimal number.

A real number does have decimal points. An example of a decimal number would be 3.142. Real numbers can also be referred to as 'float'. They are used to store data that could be a decimal or a fraction. For example, a program that stored the test scores of a class of students could have decimal numbers, as a student may gain half a mark for a question. A mark such as 9.5 out of 10 would need to be stored as a real number.

Numbers stored in a variable can be defined as an integer or real. A variable can also be converted to an integer or real if it is set as another data type initially. How this is done will depend on the programming language used.

Character

Character is a data type that holds just one character. Even though a string can hold just one character, it is more efficient to store a single character in a character data type. This is because a string may have a minimum number of bytes allocated for that data type, for example 4 bytes, so a single character would still be stored in 4 bytes of data. In contrast, a character data type will store the single character in 1 byte of data. An example of using a character could be storing M or F to represent if a person is male or female.

Boolean

A Boolean data type is one that will hold two values only, such as true/false or yes/no. When we know that an instance only has two values, Boolean is the best data type to use.

An example of Boolean data would be if a program stored data about whether a student has passed an exam or not. A variable named 'pass' could store the value yes or no.

11.04 Basic principles of programming

KEY TERM

Algorithm – a set of instructions to solve a problem.

Sequence – instructions that occur one after the other in a particular order.

Executed – a program that is run.

Selection – making a choice or a decision in a program.

Iteration – repeating instructions in a program.

Condition – a state in a program that will be met or not met.

Sequence

In an **algorithm** there are a number of basic programming principles that you need to be aware of. Having a good understanding of these principles will improve your programming skills.

In an algorithm, each instruction is written one after the other. This is called a **sequence**. Most computers handle instructions one at a time, so most programs are written as a sequence. A sequence can contain any number of steps but they have to be **executed** in the correct order:

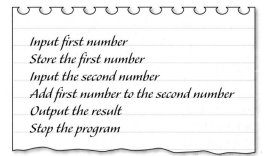

Input first number
Store the first number
Input the second number
Add first number to the second number
Output the result
Stop the program

If any of these steps were written out of order then the result of the algorithm may not be the same. Therefore, sequence is a vital principle of programming.

Selection

When creating a program it may be necessary to create a way to follow different paths through the program. Creating the ability to choose the path to follow in a program is called

selection. Selection is the process of making a decision in a program. In a selection a question is asked and then the correct path is taken depending on the answer.

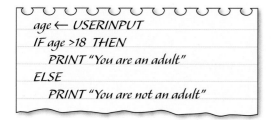

```
age ← USERINPUT
IF age >18 THEN
    PRINT "You are an adult"
ELSE
    PRINT "You are not an adult"
```

IF...THEN...ELSE is a common structure used to create selection in a program.

Iteration

Sometimes in a program there will be some instructions that need to be repeated. To repeat instructions we put them in a loop and this is referred to as **iteration**. There are two main types of loop that can be created, a counting loop and a condition loop. A counting loop repeats a set of instructions a set number of time. This loop will print 'Happy' five times:

```
FOR 5 loops:
    PRINT "Happy"
ENDFOR
```

A condition loop repeats a set of instructions until a condition is met:

```
Me ← "Happy"
REPEAT:
    PRINT Me
UNTIL Me = "Sad"
```

This will keep printing 'Happy' until the variable Me becomes 'Sad'.

A programmer has to make the decision which kind of iteration loop to use to repeat the instructions. If they want to repeat a set of instruction a defined number of times then they would use a counting loop. If they want to repeat a set of instructions until a **condition** is met or a condition stops being met then they would use a condition loop.

Totalling

It may be necessary to keep a running total in a program. For example, if we had a program that was a quiz, each time the user gets a question correct the score is updated. A variable to store the score would be created. This variable may originally be set to 0. Each time a user gets a question correct 2 is added to the score. This is done by taking the current value that is in the variable and adding 2 to it.

We would define the variable:

```
score ← 0
```

Then we would add a value of 2 to the score each time a question is correct:

$$score \leftarrow score + 2$$

By referring to the name of the variable in the calculation, it will take the value currently stored in 'score' and add 2 to it.

Counting

It may be necessary to keep a count of the amount of times something occurs in a program. For example, if we had a program that allowed a teacher to enter marks for a class, we may want to count how many marks they enter. Counting works in a very similar way to totalling. A variable to store the count would be created. This variable may be originally set to 0. Each time a process occurs 1 is added to the count. This is done by taking the current value that is in the variable and adding 1 to it. For example:

We would define the variable:

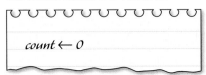

$$count \leftarrow 0$$

We then add a value of 1 to the count each time a process (such as entering a mark) occurs:

$$count \leftarrow count + 1$$

11.05 Using predefined routines

SYLLABUS CHECK

Use predefined procedures/functions.

KEY TERM

Predefined function – a pre-programmed set of instructions that return a value.
Library – a store of pre-programmed instructions that can be imported into a program.
Predefined procedure – a pre-programmed set of instructions that do not return a value.

Most programming languages have **predefined functions** that you can use as a programmer. These are functions that cover tasks that programmers commonly use such as converting integers to strings and file handling. They can be built into the language or imported from a **library**. These functions are great because we don't have to code them ourselves and they are pre-tested so we know they work.

Predefined procedures are the same except that they do not return a value like a function does. An example of a predefined procedure could be a 'clear the screen' command that would clear whatever is currently displayed when running the program.

11.06 Using an array

> **KEY TERM**
>
> **Array** – a store of data values that are all related and of the same data type.
> **Element** – an individual data location in an array.

What is an array?

> **SYLLABUS CHECK**
>
> Declare the size of one-dimensional arrays, for example: A[1:n].
> Show understanding of the use of a variable as an index in an array.

An **array** is a way of storing data that is all related and of the same type e.g. a list of the names of the students in your class could be stored in an array. Each item that is stored in an array can be accessed by referring to its location within the array.

If we wanted to store the highest scores that a player achieves in a game, we could do this in an array. An example of an array storing high scores would be:

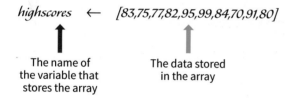

Figure 11.02 Example of an array storing high scores

Each individual item in the array has a location that can be pointed to. One important thing to note is that in most programing languages the locations start at 0 and not 1. For example the data in location 3 of the array in Figure 11.02 would be 82. Each of the individual items in an array is called an **element**.

Creating an array

In order to be able to store the high scores in an array we would need to carry out the following steps:

1 Give the variable that will store the array a name, for example highscores.

2 Set the number of elements the array will hold. This is called specifying the dimension of the array.

3 Define the type of data the array will hold. This is called specifying the data type. This step is not needed in some programming languages.

155

One important thing to note is that once we have defined the size (dimension) of an array, it normally cannot be changed.

Once we have created an array we can then write data to the array and read data from it.

Reading to and writing from arrays

We can ask a program to **read** certain elements in an array. To do this we would need to ask the program to output the data in location in an array. The program will read the data in this location in the array and output it for us to see. The following pseudocode outputs data elements from the array in Figure 11.02:

```
PRINT highscores(3)
PRINT highscores(8)
PRINT highscores(0)
```

The output would be the fourth, ninth and first elements: 82, 91 and 83. We can ask a program to **write** elements to an array. To do this we state the data location in the array that we want to write data to, followed by the data. The following pseudocode writes the high score of 90 to the second element location in the array:

```
highscores(1) ← 90
```

If the array already held a value in this element that value would be overwritten with the new value. This would mean that the current value in location 1 of the array in Figure 11.02 (75) would be overwritten with 90.

To learn more about pseudocode, see Chapter 12.

TEST YOURSELF

If we want to overwrite the first element in the high scores array with the data '99', what would the pseudocode be for this?

We can also use a variable to read data from or write data to an array. We can do this by replacing the element number with the variable name. An example of reading data from our high scores array, using a variable, would be:

```
PRINT highscores(count)
```

If the variable 'count' held the value 3, this would output the data from the fourth element in the array (82).

An example of writing data to our high scores array, using a variable, would be:

```
highscores(count) ← 75
```

If the variable 'count' still held the value 3, this would overwrite the data in the fourth element in the array (82) with the value 75.

Reading to and writing from arrays using loops

To read or write multiple values with an array we can use a FOR ... TO ... NEXT loop.

SYLLABUS CHECK

Read or write values in an array using a FOR ... TO ... NEXT loop.

A FOR ... TO ... NEXT loop will read values from or write values to an array for a set number of times:

```
FOR count ← 0 TO 3:
    PRINT highscores(count)
NEXT count
```

The 'count' variable used refers to the element number that is currently being read. It begins at 0 and when it gets to NEXT count it will increase by 1, till it gets to 3. Therefore this loop would read and output elements 0, 1, 2 and 3. With our high scores array, this loop would output the values: 83, 75, 77 and 82.

An example of using a FOR ... TO ... NEXT loop to write values to an array would be:

```
FOR count ← 0 TO 3:
    highscores(count) ← USERINPUT
NEXT count
```

With our high scores array, this FOR... TO... NEXT loop would write the value input to the relevant element. It would start with writing the first input to element 0 and keep repeating till it had written to element three. If we input the numbers 75, 77, 90 and 99 our high scores array would now look like this:

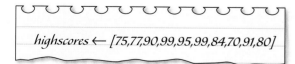

```
highscores ← [75,77,90,99,95,99,84,70,91,80]
```

157

The program does not necessarily start at element 0 each time when reading and writing data values. If the loop started with:

The program would read or write element 2 through to element 7.

To learn more about FOR … TO … NEXT loops, see Chapter 12.

Why do we use arrays?

Arrays are very useful and have several advantages for programmers:

- They store many data values under one name. This means we do not have to use or remember many variable names.
- We can easily find an item of data by specifying its element number.
- We can easily read or write many values by using a FOR … TO … NEXT loop.

Arrays also have some disadvantages:

- Once defined, the size of the array cannot normally be changed. This can be wasteful of memory if we don't use all the array's elements to hold data.
- Arrays can only hold data of one data type (the type specified when the array is defined).

Multi-dimensional arrays

The arrays we have been using are called one-dimensional arrays. This is because they only contain one set of data. Arrays can be of more than one dimension. A two-dimensional array is an arrays that holds two sets of data. An example of a two-dimensional array would be:

Multi-dimensional arrays are not part of the syllabus that you need to know. This information has been included to help you to understand the concept of an array and that they can be expanded to hold more than one set of data.

Summary

- A variable is a storage location that contains data that can be changed throughout the execution of a program.

- A constant is a storage location that contains a value that will never change.

- A string is a series of characters or symbols.

- An integer is a whole number with no decimal point.

- A real number is a number that does have a decimal point.

- Character is a data type that holds just one character.

- A Boolean data type is one that will hold two values only.

- A sequence is a set of instructions that occur one after the other in a specific order.

- Selection is the process of making a decision in a program.

- Iteration means repeating instructions in a loop. A counting loop repeats a set number of times and a condition loop repeats till a condition is met.

- Totalling is the process of keeping a running total of values in a program.

- Counting is the process of keeping a running count of how many times something happens in a program.

- A predefined routine is a pre-programmed set of instructions that can be used in a program. They are often stored in a library or built into the programming language:

  - A predefined function will return a value.

  - A predefined procedure will not return a value.

- An array is a way of storing data that is all related and of the same type. Each item that is stored in an array can be accessed by referring to its location within the array.

- Each of the individual items in an array is called an element.

- In order to create an array we need to name the variable that will store it, set the number of elements we want to hold and define the data type.

- An advantage of arrays is that they can store many data values under one name.

- A disadvantage of arrays is that once the size of the array is defined it cannot be changed. This can be wasteful of memory if we don't use all the array's elements to hold data.

Exam-style questions

1 Explain the difference between a variable and a constant. Give an example of   (2 marks)
   when you would use each.

2 A programmer would like to store the following data:

   a the user's name   (1 mark)

   b the user's age   (1 mark

   c the user's gender   (1 mark

   d the user's quiz score.   (1 mark

   Give the most suitable data type for each item of data they want to store.

3 A teacher wants to work out the average test score for a class. They want to count and
   total the number of marks they enter to calculate the average.

   a Explain how they would do this.   (5 marks)

   b The teacher wants to enter marks till they have no more marks to enter. (2 marks)
       They do not currently know how many marks they will need to enter.
       Which loop structure would they use to repeat the process of entering marks
       and why?

4 Explain why sequence is important when creating a program.   (1 mark)

5 State one reason why a programmer would use an array.   (2 marks)

6 A teacher wants to create a program that will allow them to write exam scores   (4 marks)
   for a class to an array. There are 15 students in the class. Write a suitable
   pseudocode solution that will allow the teacher to do this.

7 When creating an array, what are the two main things that we need to do?   (2 marks)

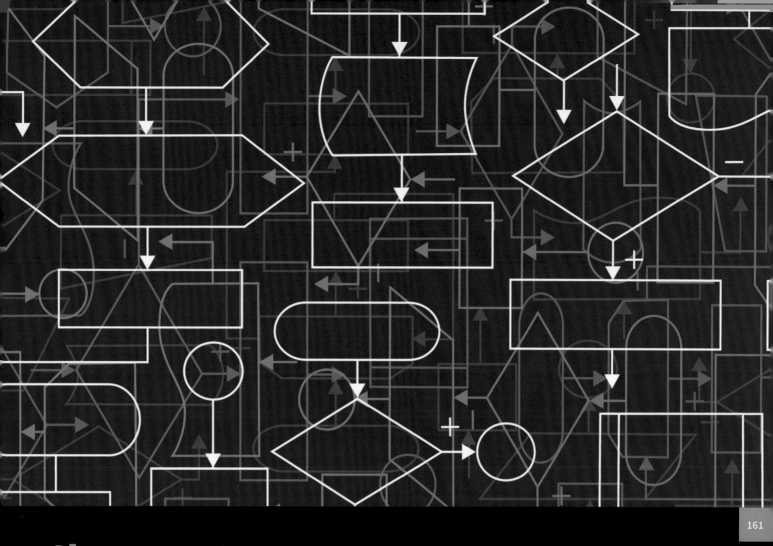

Chapter 12:
Pseudocode and Flowcharts

Learning objectives

By the end of this chapter you will be able to:

- use pseudocode and flowcharts to assign a value to a variable
- use pseudocode and flowcharts to create conditional statements
- use pseudocode and flowcharts to create loop structures
- use pseudocode and flowcharts to input and output values
- use pseudocode and flowcharts to total and count values.

12.01 Introduction

Pseudocode and flowcharts are tools that a programmer may use to help design a program, or understand one that already exists. This chapter examines how we can use them.

Many of the programming concepts discussed in this chapter are described in more detail in Chapter 11.

12.02 Pseudocode

Pseudocode is a way of describing what happens in a computer program. It is a list of instructions that show how the program will work. Pseudocode is set out with the same structure as a programming language, but it is not a programming language in itself. Pseudocode can be used to show people who do not know a particular programming language how the program works. Additionally, programmers can use it to plan and design programs.

> **KEY TERM**
>
> **Syntax** – the rules of a language.

There is not a standard **syntax** for pseudocode, but there are some commonly followed conventions. This means that pseudocode written by one programmer can be easily understood by another.

Pseudocode covers a range of programming elements:

- comments
- variables
- arrays
- selection
- iteration
- input and output
- procedures and functions.

Comments

In pseudocode comments are written to state what a particular line or section of code is for. A commented line starts with a hash symbol:

```
# this is a comment!
# this variable holds the player's score
```

It is just as important to comment our code when writing pseudocode as it is when writing real code. Without comments, any code can be difficult to understand. We should be aware of writing too few or too many comments in our code. Too few comments can make it harder to understand a program. Too many comments can make it difficult for us to find what we are looking for in a program.

Variables

> **SYLLABUS CHECK**
>
> Understand and use pseudocode for assignment, using ←.

A **variable** is a named location in memory that holds a data value. The data held in a variable may change repeatedly throughout the running of a program. In pseudocode variables are shown using the format in Figure 12.01.

Variable – a named location in memory that holds a data value.

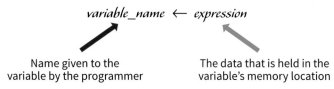

Name given to the variable by the programmer

The data that is held in the variable's memory location

Figure 12.01 Variables shown in pseudocode

We can assign a value to the variable:

```
score ← 0      # create a variable named score, assigned the value 0
```

A variable's data type is not usually specified in pseudocode. If required, a comment can be included stating the type to be assigned.

To learn more about variables, see Chapter 11.

Arrays

An **array** is a data structure that holds a collection of values of the same data type. In pseudocode an array is declared by stating the array name. Data can be assigned by placing the values in between parentheses []. An array can also be left blank so data is assigned during the program.

Array – a data structure that holds a collection of values of the same data type.

```
highscores ← []                          # create an empty array
playernames ← [Sarah, Vikram, Amy]       # create an array with 3 values assigned
```

The arrays above are one-dimensional arrays. This type of array holds one set of related values.

Programmers can also use two-dimensional arrays. This type of array holds two separate sets of related values. In pseudocode two-dimensional arrays are declared by using two sets of parentheses, one for each set of data:

```
# create an array with two data sets
namesandscores ← [Sarah, Vikram, Amy] [100, 88, 72]
```

Multi-dimensional arrays are not part of the syllabus that you need to know. This information has been included to help you to understand the concept of an array and that they can be expanded to hold more than one set of data.

To learn more about arrays, see Chapter 11.

Counting

> **SYLLABUS CHECK**
>
> Use the following commands and statements: counting (e.g. Count ← Count + 1).

Sometimes in a program we need to keep a record of how many times something has happened. The method used to do this is called a count. A variable is used to hold the value of the current count. A count may be added to or subtracted from. In pseudocode a count is done using the format:

```
count ← count + 1        # add 1 to the value of count
count ← count – 1        # subtracts 1 from the value of count
count ← count + number   # add the value of a variable named number to the value of count
```

If we begin our count at 0 we would start by assigning a variable named count with the value 0:

```
count ← 0
```

We might want to keep a record of how many times we run a particular set of instruction in a program. Within this set of instructions we would have the line of code:

```
count ← count + 1
```

This would take the value stored in count (initially 0) and add 1 to it. The value stored in count would then become 1. The next time the set of instructions is run it would take the value stored in count (now 1) and add 1 to it. The value then stored in count would be 2.

Totalling

> **SYLLABUS CHECK**
>
> Use the following commands and statements: totalling (SUM ← SUM + Number).

Totalling is the process of keeping a running total of certain values in a program. A variable is used to hold the value of the total. In pseudocode totalling is done using the format:

```
total ← total + number      # the total is incremented by the value of the number
```

We would start by assigning a variable named total with the value 0:

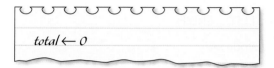

```
total ← 0
```

We may want to keep a running total for an item in a program. We would add a related value to the total whenever it is input:

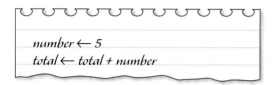

```
number ← 5
total ← total + number
```

This would take the value held in the variable with the name 'total' (initially 0) and add to it the value that is held in the variable with the name 'number'. The value held in total will then become 5.

At a further point in the program another value needs to be added to the total:

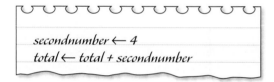

```
secondnumber ← 4
total ← total + secondnumber
```

This would take the value held in total (now 5) and add to it the value that is held in secondnumber (this is 4). The value held in total will then become 9.

To learn more about counting and totalling, see Chapter 11.

Selection

SYLLABUS CHECK

Use the following conditional statements:
- IF … THEN … ELSE … ENDIF
- CASE … OF … OTHERWISE … ENDCASE.

Selection in a program allows a program to follow different paths. The choice of path is determined using **conditions**. A path is followed depending on the whether a particular condition is met or not. For example, a message of congratulations might be output if an exam score was high enough to pass. Another message to 'try again' might be output if the score was too low. Selection can be described in pseudocode using IF statements and CASE statements.

KEY TERM

Condition – a state in a program that will be met or not met.

Selection – a statement that represents choice in an algorithm.

IF statements

IF statements allow a programmer to define several paths through a program. A Condition will determine which path is followed. IF statements take the form IF ... THEN ... ELSE ... ENDIF:

The exam score selection example described above could be written in pseudocode as:

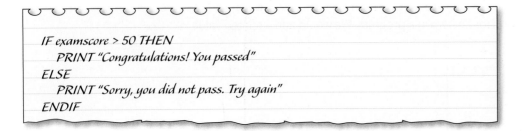

```
IF examscore > 50 THEN
    PRINT "Congratulations! You passed"
ELSE
    PRINT "Sorry, you did not pass. Try again"
ENDIF
```

This means that if the value of examscore is greater than 50, the congratulations message is output. For any exam score less than or equal to 50, the 'try again' message would be output.

This example could be extended to include an extra message for especially high marks:

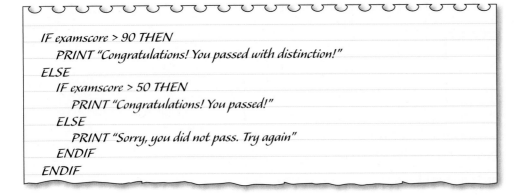

```
IF examscore > 90 THEN
    PRINT "Congratulations! You passed with distinction!"
ELSE
    IF examscore > 50 THEN
        PRINT "Congratulations! You passed!"
    ELSE
        PRINT "Sorry, you did not pass. Try again"
    ENDIF
ENDIF
```

CASE statements

When many possible paths exist, using IF statements can make code complicated. Another selection method that can be used is the CASE statement. CASE is used when specific discrete data values are used, not for those that might be in a range. For example:

- If examscore can be one of 1, 2, 3, 4 or 5 use CASE because specific values are considered.
- If examscore is greater than 50 use IF because a large possible range of values are considered.

When dealing with many paths with specific condition values, using CASE allows for simpler, easier to read code. In pseudocode, CASE statements take the form CASE ... OF ... OTHERWISE ... ENDCASE:

```
CASE examscore OF
1: PRINT "Sorry, you did not pass"
2: PRINT "Sorry you did not pass, but you were close"
3: PRINT "You passed, but only just"
4: PRINT "You passed with a decent score!"
5: PRINT "You passed with distinction!"
OTHERWISE
    PRINT "Your score was not recognised"
ENDCASE
```

To learn more about selection, see Chapter 11.

Iteration

Sometimes a programmer may need to make a section of code run repeatedly. For example, if we need to enter a series of numbers, the input code will need to be repeated until all numbers have been entered. **Iteration** can be implemented using three types of loop:

- **count-controlled loops** using FOR

- **condition-controlled loops** using WHILE

- **condition-controlled loops** using REPEAT.

KEY TERM

Iteration – where a section of code is run repeatedly.

Count-controlled loop – iteration that is performed a stated number of times.

Condition-controlled loop – iteration that continues until, or while, a condition is met.

FOR loops

A FOR loop is used when the loop is to be repeated a fixed number of times. As the number of times is fixed, we say the loop is 'count-controlled'. We need to increase a counter each time the loop is performed. The loop ends when the counter matches the number of times the loop is to be repeated.

In pseudocode a count-controlled loop takes the form FOR ... TO ... NEXT:

```
FOR count ← 0 TO 4:
    PRINT "Type in a number"
    number ← USERINPUT
    total ← total + number
NEXT count
```

This loop will iterate five times. This is because the first value of count is 0 and the last value of count is 4, giving five iterations. This will allow the user to enter five numbers.

TEST YOURSELF

What else will the program do?

WHILE loops

A WHILE loop is used when the programmer does not know exactly how many times the loop will need to be performed. The loop continues while a condition is being met. In pseudocode a WHILE loop takes the form WHILE ... DO ... ENDWHILE:

```
WHILE hungry = TRUE DO
    PRINT "I'm hungry"
    hungry ← USERINPUT
ENDWHILE
```

It is possible that the code in a WHILE loop is never run. This is because the condition is tested at the beginning of the loop. If the condition is not met then the loop will not run and the program will continue.

TEST YOURSELF

What will this program do?

REPEAT loops

A REPEAT loop can also be used when the programmer does not know exactly how many times the loop will need to be performed. The loop ends when a condition is met. In pseudocode a REPEAT loop takes the form REPEAT ... UNTIL:

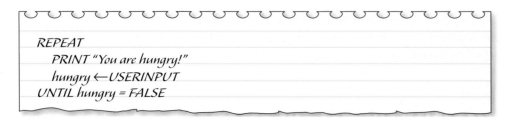

```
REPEAT
    PRINT "You are hungry!"
    hungry ← USERINPUT
UNTIL hungry = FALSE
```

This loop repeats until the user says they are not hungry (the input is FALSE).

Code in a REPEAT loop is always run at least once. This is because the condition is not tested until the code in the loop has run the first time.

TEST YOURSELF

If a teacher has a set of 10 exam marks to enter, which type of loop should they use? Explain why.

To learn more about iteration, see Chapter 11.

Input and output

SYLLABUS CHECK

Use the following commands and statements: INPUT and OUTPUT (e.g. READ and PRINT).

Most programs will need to allow a user to enter data and will also have to present data to the user. This is known as input and output. Data may also be input from or output to a file.

USERINPUT

An input from a user in pseudocode takes the form USERINPUT:

```
studentname ← USERINPUT
```

This instruction waits for the user to type something in and then assigns that data to the named variable.

OUTPUT

An output to a user in pseudocode takes the form PRINT:

```
PRINT "Hello!"        # outputs a string (the text Hello)
PRINT highscore       # outputs a variable's value
```

READLINE

Data can also be input from a file. When using pseudocode, the programmer must remember to specify the filename. Reading from a file is described in pseudocode as:

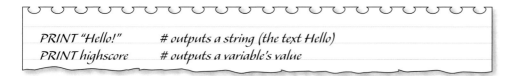

```
name ← READLINE(filename, record number)
```

This would read the data from whatever filename and record number was stated and hold it in the variable 'name'.

We have a file called computer_science_students.txt that holds the names of a class of students who study Computer Science. The data in the file is shown in Table 12.01.

Table 12.01

Record number	Student name
0	Amy
1	Jan
2	Bosire
3	Amaan
4	Seema

The pseudocode to read the third record into a variable would be:

```
name ← READLINE(computer_science_students.txt, 2)
```

The variable 'name' would now hold the value 'Bosire'. The number 2 is used for the READLINE command because the record count starts at 0. This means the first name in the file is 0, the second is 1, the third is 2, etc.

WRITELINE

Data can also be output to a file. WRITELINE overwrites a line in a file. If no line exists, a new one is created. As with READLINE, the programmer must remember to specify the filename. Writing to a file is described in pseudocode as:

```
WRITELINE (filename, record number, value)
```

We can add a new student to the data in Table 12.01:

```
new_student ← "Francesca"
WRITELINE(computing_students.txt, 5, new_student)
```

This would result in the data file now having the contents shown in Table 12.02.

Table 12.02

Record number	Student name
0	Amy
1	Jan
2	Bosire
3	Amaan
4	Seema
5	Francesca

WRITELINE can also be used to remove a value:

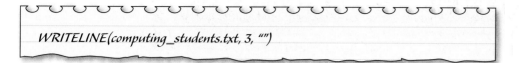

```
WRITELINE(computing_students.txt, 3, "")
```

The contents of the file would now be as shown in Table 12.03.

Table 12.03

Record number	Student name
0	Amy
1	Jan
2	Bosire
3	
4	Seema
5	Francesca

Procedures

Sometimes sections of code are used more than once in a program. When this occurs, procedures and functions should be used. This is to avoid the same set of code being typed repeatedly.

KEY TERM

Procedure – a small section of code that can be run repeatedly from different parts of the program.

Function – a procedure that returns a value.

Procedures are sections of code that can be reused. They do not return a value. In pseudocode, a procedure is named and takes the form PROCEDURE … ENDPROCEDURE:

```
PROCEDURE Menu
    PRINT "1. Continue"
    PRINT "2. Quit"
ENDPROCEDURE
```

In pseudocode, procedures are run using the CALL statement:

```
CALL Menu
```

171

Functions

Functions are similar to procedures. The difference is that functions have one or more values put into them and one or more values are given back to main program at the end. We call this 'passing values' in and out of the function.

In pseudocode, a function takes the following form:

```
FUNCTION(values to be passed in)
    ...
    RETURN (values to be passed out)
ENDFUNCTION
```

The following function performs a calculation on a number and returns the answer:

```
FUNCTION Fahrenheit_to_celsius (fahrenheit):
    celsius ← ((fahrenheit -32) * (5/9))
    RETURN Celsius
ENDFUNCTION
```

In pseudocode, functions are run using the CALL statement:

```
fahrenheit ← 32
CALL Fahrenheit_to_celsius (fahrenheit)
```

To learn more about procedures and functions, see Chapter 11.

12.03 Flowcharts

Pseudocode is a text-based method of designing programs. Flowcharts are a graphical method of designing programs. They allow the designer to see a visual representation of a problem. They are also useful in understanding the logic of complicated problems.

Flowcharts are usually drawn using some standard symbols, shown in Table 12.04.

Table 12.04

Purpose	Symbol
Start and end of the program	Start Stop
Computational steps or processing function of a program	
Input or output (of data)	
Decision making and branching	
Direction of flow	→

Flowcharting guidelines

The following are some guidelines for flowcharting:

- All necessary requirements should be listed in logical order.

- The flowchart should be clear, neat and easy to follow.

- There should not be any room for uncertainty in understanding the flowchart.

- The usual direction of the flow of a procedure or system is from left to right or top to bottom.

- Only one flow line should come from a symbol, unless it is a decision symbol.

Figure 12.02 Computational steps

- Only one flow line should enter a decision symbol, but two or three flow lines, one for each possible answer, may leave the decision symbol.

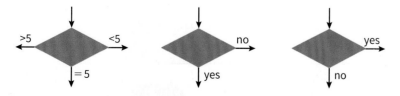

Figure 12.03 Decision symbol with a single flow line entering and two or three leaving the symbol

- Only one flow line is used for a terminal symbol. Some flowcharts may spread over many pages, making it essential to know where a process begins and ends.

Figure 12.04 Terminal symbols for the start and end of a program

- Ensure that the flowchart has a logical start and finish.
- It is useful to test if a flowchart is correct by working through it with simple test data.

Writing a flowchart for an algorithm

SYLLABUS CHECK

Produce an algorithm for a given problem (either in the form of pseudocode or flowchart).

Draw a flowchart to find the average of two numbers.

Algorithm:

Input: two numbers, aNumber and secNumber

Output: the average of aNumber and secNumber

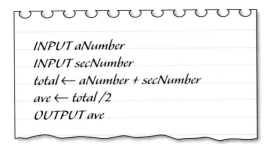

The flowchart for this algorithm is shown in Figure 12.05.

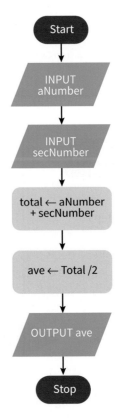

Figure 12.05 Complete flowchart for an algorithm

Selection in flowcharts

Selection using IF statements is represented in flowcharts using a decision box.

Algorithm:

Input: number

Decision: Is the number positive or negative?

Output: Number is positive, Number is negative

> INPUT number
> DECISION Is number greater than 0?
> IF YES OUTPUT Number is positive
> IF NO OUTPUT Number is negative

The flowchart for this algorithm is shown in Figure 12.06.

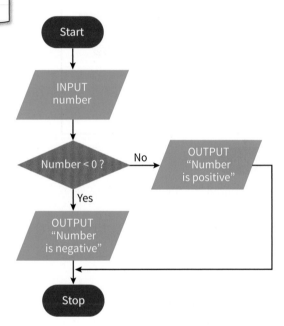

175

Figure 12.06 IF statement represented in a flowchart

CASE statements can also be represented. In practice CASE statements are represented in flowcharts in the same manner as IF statements.

Algorithm:

Input: number for animal

Output: dog, cat, horse

> INPUT numAnimal
> CASE numAnimal OF
> 1: OUTPUT dog
> 2: OUTPUT cat
> 3: OUTPUT horse
> OTHERWISE
>   OUTPUT Out of range

The flowchart for this algorithm is shown in Figure 12.07.

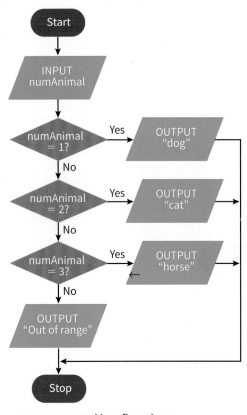

Figure 12.07 CASE statement represented in a flowchart

Iteration in flowcharts

Each of the types of iteration can be drawn in a flowchart.

Figure 12.08 shows a FOR loop.

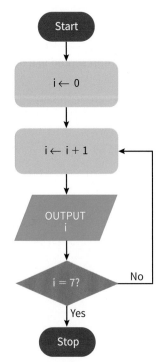

Figure 12.08 FOR loop represented in a flowchart

What does the program shown in Figure 12.08 do?

Figure 12.09 shows an WHILE loop. The symbol ! can be used to say that a value is not equal to something.

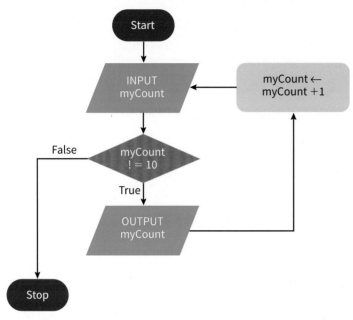

Figure 12.09 WHILE loop represented in a flowchart

What will the program shown in Figure 12.09 do?

Figure 12.10 shows a REPEAT loop.

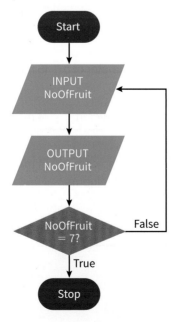

Figure 12.10 REPEAT loop represented in a flowchart

TEST YOURSELF

Design a flowchart algorithm for finding the area of a rectangle.

Hints:

- Define the inputs and the outputs.
- Define the steps.
- Draw the flowchart.

Summary

- Pseudocode and flowcharts are tools that a programmer may use to help design a program, or understand one that already exists.
- Pseudocode is a text based list of instructions that specify how a program is to work.
- Pseudocode is set out with the same structure as a programming language.
- Programmers can use Pseudocode to plan and design programs.
- Pseudocode equivalents exist for comments, variables, arrays, selection, iteration, input and output, functions and procedures.
- Flowcharts are a graphical method of designing algorithms.
- Flowcharts allow the designer to see a visual representation of a problem.
- Flowcharts are useful in understanding the logic of complicated problems.
- Flowcharts use symbols to represent processes, selection, iteration, input and output.

Exam-style questions

1   Explain why comments should be used in pseudocode.   (2 marks)

2   Explain why flowcharts are a useful design tool.   (2 marks)

3   What symbol is used in a flowchart to represent a decision?   (1 mark)

4   Design a pseudocode algorithm that will calculate the area and perimeter of a   (5 marks)
    triangle. The user must choose which answer they want to be output.

5   Design a flowchart algorithm that makes sure a user only enters an integer in   (4 marks)
    the range 1 to 10.

6   Design a flowchart algorithm for a simple drinks machine. The user can choose   (4 marks)
    from tea, coffee, hot chocolate, orange juice and apple juice. If the user inputs
    a drink that is not listed an error message should be displayed.

7   Amy has been asked to design an algorithm for a very large program.   (3 marks)
    Which design tool, pseudocode or flowchart, do you think would be most
    suitable? Explain your answer.

Chapter 13:
Algorithm Design and Problem-solving

Learning objectives

By the end of this chapter you will:

- understand that every computer system is made up of sub-systems
- be able to use top-down design and structure diagrams
- be able to explain standard methods of solution including pseudocode and flowcharts
- be able to suggest and apply suitable test data
- understand the need for validation and verification checks to be made on input data
- be able to use trace tables to find the values of variables at each step in an algorithm
- be able to identify errors in given algorithms and suggest ways of removing these errors
- be able to produce an algorithm for a given problem.

13.01 Computer systems and sub-systems

We often think of a computer system as one single system that performs tasks. However, it a system that is made up of sub-systems, that can often be made up of sub-systems too.

For example, a smartphone does not just have one system that allows us to make telephone calls. It has many sub-systems that are part of this. These sub-systems manage:

- inputs and outputs via the touch screen
- file storage
- radio transmissions.

These sub-systems also have sub-systems of their own:

- The input/output sub-system has sub-systems to update the display and detect user input.
- The file handling sub-system has sub-systems to write data to storage and read data from storage.
- The radio transmissions sub-system has sub-systems to manage outgoing and incoming transmissions.

Each system and sub-system is created from a series of instructions that tell the computer what to do. These steps are known as an algorithm.

KEY TERM

Subroutine – a short section of code within a program.

Library routine – a commonly used function that is available to a programmer.

Algorithm designers can also make use of **subroutines** and **library routines** to simplify programs.

A subroutine is a small section of a program that is part of a larger program. For example, a game might include a subroutine to display a high-score table.

A library routine is a collection of small, commonly used programs and subroutines that can be used in another program. For example, a library routine could create random numbers. The main program can use this library routine whenever a random number needs to be created. This kind of library routine could be used to simulate throwing dice in a game.

TEST YOURSELF

Research two library routines for a particular programming language. What can they be used for?

13.02 Top-down design and structure diagrams

Algorithms can be designed in several ways and different programmers prefer some methods above others. Algorithm design methods include:

* top-down design

* structure diagrams

* flowcharts

* pseudocode.

KEY TERM

Top-down design – a design process where an overall task is broken down into smaller tasks.

Decomposition – the process of breaking down a large task into smaller tasks.

Structure diagram – a diagram that shows tasks that have been broken down and how they relate to each other.

Module – an individual section of code that can be used by other programs.

When designing a computer system we refer to the system as a 'complex problem'. The sub-systems within a system are referred to as 'sub-problems'. **Top-down design** is a design method that involves taking a complex problem and breaking it down into smaller sub-problems. These sub-problems can often be broken down into even smaller sub-problems. This process is known as **decomposition**.

The complex problem of the smartphone system was broken down into sub-problems:

* a sub-system to manage inputs and outputs via the touch screen

* a sub-system to manage file storage

* a sub-system to manage radio transmissions.

This can be represented diagrammatically as a **structure diagram** (also known as a top-down diagram). A structure diagram shows how each system (problem) and sub-system (sub-problem) is broken down from top to bottom. Each box is referred to as a **module**.

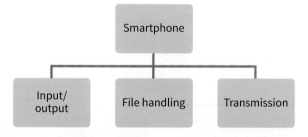

Figure 13.01 A simple structure diagram of sub-systems for a smartphone

Once each sub-problem has been identified, it can then be broken down into smaller sub-problems. These sub-problems are represented in the structure diagram with their own modules:

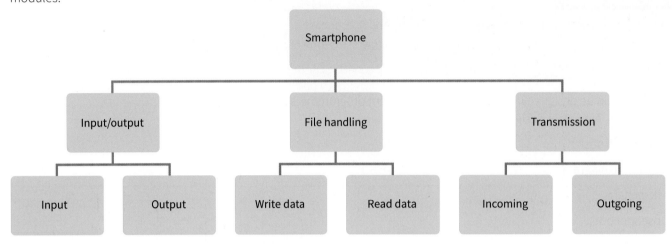

Figure 13.02 A structure diagram of sub-systems within sub-systems in a smartphone

The decomposition process can be continued until each problem is broken down into its simplest state. A designer starts at the top and breaks down each problem and sub-problem, hence the term 'top-down design'.

A good way to approach top-down design is to follow these steps:

- To solve a large problem, break the problem into several smaller tasks and work on each task separately.

- To solve each task, treat it as a new problem that can be broken down into smaller problems.

- Repeat this process with each new task until each can be solved without the need for any further decomposition.

A finance office needs an algorithm to calculate weekly pay. The algorithm needs to determine how many normal hours and how many overtime hours each employee works. Overtime is paid at 1.5 times the normal hourly rate. An employee's total weekly pay should be output at the end.

A top-down solution might look like the one in Figure 13.03.

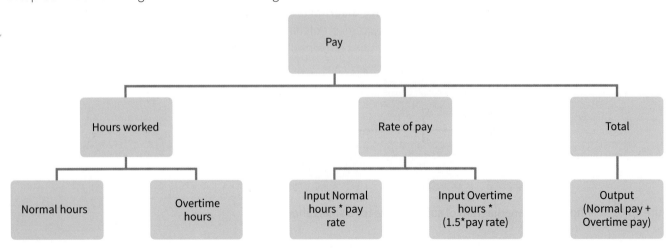

Figure 13.03 A structure diagram of an algorithm to calculate an employee's weekly pay

From this top-down design a suitable algorithm could be created to calculate the correct weekly pay for each employee.

Using top-down design to design an algorithm has several benefits:

- Algorithms can be developed quickly as more than one person can work to solve the problem.
  - Different designers can work on modules individually then bring the sub-problems together at the end.
  - Once each module has been designed, they can be given to different programmers to code. This speeds up the development of the program.
  - Each programmer can be given a module that is suitable for their area of expertise. For example, an expert in interface design could be given the interface modules and an expert in file-handling could be given the file-handling modules.
  - As each module is a shorter program they are easier to write, test and de-bug than the full system.
- The structure diagram shows how different modules relate to each other. This can be important in helping to visualise how a program works.
- Modules can be re-used in different programs that require the same structure.
- Structure diagrams make it easier for another designer to understand the logic of an algorithm.

13.03 Standard methods of solution

There are a number of ways of designing a solution to a problem, in the form of an algorithm. The two main methods of solution are flowcharts and pseudocode.

Flowcharts

A flowchart is a way of representing the structure and flow of an algorithm. Flowcharts show the sequence, selection and iteration within an algorithm. Individual steps (sequence) are represented, as are the different paths (selection) and loops (iteration) that might be followed whilst working through the algorithm.

Table 13.01

Advantages of using flowcharts	Disadvantages of using flowcharts
The sequence of steps can easily be seen	They can take a lot of time to produce
Paths through the algorithm can be easily followed	Changes to the algorithm mean sections of the flowchart have to be re-drawn. This can take a lot of time
The logic of the algorithm (sequence, selection and iteration) can often be understood better when represented visually	Large flowcharts can become extremely complicated and difficult to follow
Flowcharts can form part of the documentation for a system, helping others to easily understand how a program works	

To learn more about flowcharts, see Chapter 12.

Pseudocode

Pseudocode is a text-based method of describing an algorithm. It looks like a programming language, but in fact it is not a programming language at all. Instead, it borrows terminology from programming languages, but it does not follow the **syntax** of any particular language.

KEY TERM

Syntax – the structure of a language.

Pseudocode is useful because it represents a half-way point between a programming language and a description of the algorithm in plain English.

A pseudocode algorithm for calculating the cost of a purchase could be:

```
discount ← 0.9
price per unit ← USERINPUT
quantity ← USERINPUT
result ← (price per unit * quantity)
IF result > 100 THEN
    result ← (result * discount)
ENDIF
PRINT result
```

TEST YOURSELF

Using the cost-calculating algorithm, determine the cost of purchasing a single item when:
1   the unit price is €75
2   the unit price is €120.

To learn more about pseudocode, see Chapter 12.

There are often a number of different ways to create a solution to a problem. Some of the ways may be effective, some may not be too effective and could be improved. In order to consider how effective a solution is we need to look at the algorithm and ask some questions:

- Could the algorithm be simplified in any way?
- Are any parts of the algorithm repeated that could be made more efficient if placed in a loop/procedure?
- Does the algorithm have any parts that are not used and therefore unnecessary?

If the answer is yes to any of the questions above then the algorithm is not the most effective way of solving the problem and we can look to improve the algorithm as a result.

13.04 Test data

SYLLABUS CHECK

Be able to suggest and apply suitable test data.

During the development of a program, and when it is complete, it is good practice to test the code to make sure it does not contain any errors (bugs). It is possible for even the simplest part of a program to contain bugs. To test a program, each section of the code is run using sample data. This sample data is known as test data.

Three types of test data should be used to make sure a program is bug-free:

- Normal (typical) data is valid data that the code would be expected to accept. For example, if an input should be an integer in the range 1–100, normal data would be any integer in that range.
- Extreme data is also valid data that the code would be expected to accept. However, the data used is at the boundary of what should be accepted. In the case of an input requiring an integer in the range 1–100, the values 1 and 100 would be considered to be extreme test data.
- Invalid (erroneous) data is data that the code should not accept. Data that should not be accepted is entered to test that the code responds correctly to such an input. For example, entering a letter when code expects an integer should result in an error message and the user being asked to re-input the data.

A program has been written that calculates sales of tickets for an outdoor festival. A customer is allowed to buy between 1 and 5 tickets. The program could be tested with the test data shown in Table 13.02.

Table 13.02

Type of test data	Examples
Typical	2 3 4
Extreme	1 5
Invalid	0 6 1.5 'y' entering nothing at all

TEST YOURSELF

Explain why each of the above data meets the criteria of normal, extreme and invalid data?

Before a program is tested a testing table is usually drawn up. A testing table should contain the headings shown in Table 13.03.

Table 13.03

Test description	Test data	Test type	Expected outcome	Actual outcome
Enter number of tickets to be bought	1	Extreme	Entry should be accepted and customer transferred to the 'confirm order' screen	Successful
Enter number of tickets to be bought	6	Invalid	Error message 'Please enter a number between 1 and 5' should display	Successful

Testing should be thorough and complete. Several examples of normal, extreme and invalid data should be entered to make sure that the code works as expected.

13.05 Validation and verification

SYLLABUS CHECK

Understand the need for validation and verification checks to be made on input data (validation could include range checks, length checks, type checks and check digits).

When we enter data it is impossible to guarantee that the data we enter is error free. When data is entered or copied from one place to another, errors can easily be introduced. It is very easy to accidently omit data, mistype data, or misread a value or word. To help prevent data entry errors, two techniques are used: validation checks and verification checks.

KEY TERM

Validation – an automatic check to make sure data is sensible and possible.

Verification – a check to see if the data entered is correct.

Validation checks

Validation checks ensure that data being entered is both sensible and possible. Table 13.04 show types of validation checks.

Table 13.04

Validation check	Description	Example data
Range check	Specifies that data entered must be numerical data in a range, for example in the range 1 to 18	5 (valid) 19 (invalid)
Presence check	Makes sure that a field has to have data entered in it, for example, when entering a new password	Any data entered (valid) Leaving it blank (invalid)
Type check	Specifies that only a certain type of data can be entered, for example, not allowing letters into a field that should only contain numbers	5 (valid) five (invalid)

Validation check	Description	Example data
Lookup	Providing the user with a drop-down list to select data. For example, when selecting an employment status, a drop-down list of the options employed, self-employed, unemployed	Anything from the list (valid) Anything else (invalid)
Length check	Specifies that data entered has to be a certain number of characters long. For example, a password needs to have 8 or more characters	p@s5w0rd (valid) l3tme1n (invalid)
Format check	Specifies that data entered has to conform to a specific format. Some pieces of data are formed of characters in a very specific order. For example, a UK vehicle registration has two letters, followed by two numbers, followed by a space, followed by three letters	MA63 SLK (valid) D15G JPT (invalid)

More than one type of validation check might be needed for a set of data. For example, a shop would apply a format check to make sure each product it sells is given a selling price in the same format. Additionally, a presence check would also be applied to make sure no product is left without a selling price.

TEST YOURSELF

A real estate agent stores data about the properties they sell. Suggest suitable validation for each data item in Table 13.05 and justify your choice.

Table 13.05

Data	Validation checks
Property type	
Number of bedrooms	
Garden	
Seller's family name	
Selling price	

Check digits

When entering a series of numbers it is easy for a user to incorrectly enter a number. A special form of validation checks that a series of numbers has been entered correctly by carrying out a series of calculations on the numbers entered.

Various methods exist and a good example is the check digit applied to International Standard Book Numbers (ISBN). Every book sold has an ISBN. This consists of a series of either 10 or 13 numbers. The check digit method for making sure that 10/13 correct numbers have been entered is known as the ISBN-13 check digit. The ISBN-13 check digit makes use of modulo-10 division. This is a method that divides a sum by 10 and uses the remainder as part of the final calculation.

Consider the ISBN number 9782053703008. With ISBN-13, the check digit is the last digit in the ISBN number. In this case the check digit is 8. This digit is removed from the number as it is used in the final check. Each remaining digit is given a value by which is it multiplied, called a 'weighting'. The values are standard and are applied to all ISBN-13 numbers. The values are 1 and 3 and they alternate from number to number as shown in Table 13.06.

Table 13.06

ISBN digit	9	7	8	2	0	5	3	7	0	3	0	0
Weighting	1	3	1	3	1	3	1	3	1	3	1	3

To calculate the check digit, carry out the following steps:

1   Multiply each digit by its weighting, then add together the result of each of the calculations:

$$(9 \times 1) + (7 \times 3) + (8 \times 1) + (2 \times 3) + (0 \times 1) + (5 \times 3) + (3 \times 1) + (7 \times 3)$$
$$+ (0 \times 1) + (3 \times 3) + (0 \times 1) + (0 \times 3)$$
$$= 9 + 21 + 8 + 6 + 0 + 15 + 3 + 21 + 0 + 9 + 0 + 0$$
$$= 92$$

2   Apply modulo-10 division to the sum to determine the remainder. Modulo-10 division means the number is divided by 10 and the remainder of this calculation is noted:

$$92 \div 10 = 9 \text{ remainder } 2$$

3   Finally, subtract the remainder from 10. The result is the check digit value:

$$10 - 2 = 8.$$

The result of the calculation matches the check digit at the end of the ISBN: they are both 8. As they match, the computer knows that the ISBN number has been entered correctly.

Check digits are also used in data transmission. To find out more about this, see Chapter 2.

Verification checks

Validation helps to make sure that data is both sensible and possible. However, validation does not ensure that the data is correct. Even if the data is reasonable and possible, it might still be incorrect.

In a range check of 1 to 10 a user may mean to enter a value of 8, but instead enter a value of 7. The value would still be accepted as it is between 1 and 10, but it is incorrect as the user meant to enter 8. **Verification** is intended to catch such errors.

There are three ways in which data can be verified; two are automated methods:

- Double entry – The user enters the data twice. The computer checks to see that both entries match. If they do not match, the user is prompted to re-enter the data again. This is often used when entering a password. It makes sure the user has set the password they wanted and has not mistyped it.

- Twin entry – Two users enter the same data separately. The computer checks to see that both entries match. If they do not match, both users are prompted to re-enter the data again.

- Proofreading – One user enters the data and a second user reads it. If it appears to be okay, the data is accepted into the system. Otherwise the second user amends the data, then submits it.

Despite the use of validation and verification, data can still be entered incorrectly. For example, it is possible for a user to enter a number or name incorrectly the same way twice. Validation and verification prevent many mistakes but it cannot stop all data entry errors from occurring.

13.06 Trace tables

SYLLABUS CHECK

Be able to use trace tables to find the value of variables at each step in an algorithm.

Sometimes when we test a program it produces unexpected results. For example, consider the following simple pseudocode algorithm for calculating the average of a set of four numbers:

```
total ← 0
count ← 0
WHILE count < 3:
    INPUT ("Enter a number") as float
    GET number
    total = total * number
    count = count + 1
END WHILE
average = total / count
PRINT ("Average = ", average)
```

A programmer converts the algorithm to code. The program is run and tested with the following data:

$$1, 2, 3$$

The total of this data is 6, which gives an average of 2 ($6 \div 3 = 2$). However, when the program is run, the average is output as 0. There is clearly an error, but where?

KEY TERM

Dry run – paper-based run through an algorithm or a program.

Trace table – a table used to trace the values of variables through the execution of a program.

To determine where errors are in code, programmers often perform what is called a **dry run** using a **trace table.** With a dry run, the programmer makes a list of all the variables in the order they appear in the code and places them in a table. A trace table for the algorithm above would look like Table 13.07.

Table 13.07

total	count	number	average

To perform the dry run, the programmer works manually through each line of code, making a note of any variable that changes value by placing that new value in a new line in the trace table. From this it can often be seen where an error is occurring as shown in Table 13.08.

Table 13.08

total	count	number	average
0			
	0		
		1	
	1		
		2	
	2		
		3	
	3		
			0

From this trace table it can be immediately seen that the error lies in the section of the algorithm that adds the input number to the total. The average is output as 0, because the total stays 0 and 0 ÷ 3 = 0.

Inspecting the algorithm reveals an incorrect line:

total = total * number

This should read:

total = total + number

When a dry run is performed again using the same data, the trace table gives the values shown in Table 13.09.

Table 13.09

total	count	number	average
0			
	0		
		1	
1			
	1		
		2	
3			
	2		
		3	
6			
	3		
			2

Trace tables are extremely useful as they can help to quickly pinpoint where an error is occurring, simply by noting where a variable holds a different value than what we expected. However, if the program has many iterations a trace table can be extremely long.

SYLLABUS CHECK

Identify errors in given algorithms and suggest ways of removing these errors.

13.07 Errors in a program

 KEY TERM

Syntax error – an error that occurs because the programmer does not use the correct language structure in a program.

Logic error – an error that causes a program to do something unexpected.

Programmers are human. Humans make mistakes. When programming, humans make two main types of mistake: **syntax errors** and **logic errors**.

Syntax errors

A syntax error occurs when a programmer does not follow the rules or structure of the language they are writing in. Syntax errors occur in various forms:

For example, in Visual Basic, a variable is declared by using the following syntax:

```
Dim noOfStudents As Integer
```

Possible syntax errors are shown in Table 13.10.

Table 13.10

Code with a syntax error	Description of error
`Dim noOfStudents`	The line is incomplete
`Dim noOfStudents As Interger`	The line contains a spelling error
`Dim Integer As noOfStudents`	The elements are in the wrong order

If a program contains a syntax error it will stop when the line containing the error is reached.

Logic errors

A logic error is an error in the code that causes the program to do something it should not, for example, produce an incorrect result to a calculation. Consider the following code, which should calculate and output an exam percentage:

```
print (score/possibleMarks) * 1000
```

In calculating the percentage, the code should multiply the result by 100. The code above multiplies by 1000. Although the code will run, it will display the wrong answer.

Other examples of logic errors include:

- Using a conditional loop where the condition is unintentionally never met would result in what we call 'an infinite loop' (it will never stop looping).
- Assigning the wrong data type to a variable, for example specifying an integer instead of a float, may result in rounded up numbers.
- Using the same variable name for different purposes within a program may mean that the variable's value changes unexpectedly.

Summary

- Computer systems consist of sub-systems. These sub-systems can have sub-systems of their own.
- Algorithms are step-by-step designs that describe how systems and sub-systems work.
- Subroutines are short sections of code within a program.
- Top-down design is a design method where a problem is broken down into smaller problems. Structure diagrams are used to show how modules fit together and relate to each other.
- Flowcharts represent the structure and flow of an algorithm.
- Pseudocode is a text-based method of describing how an algorithm works.
- Test data is used to test a program. A test table documents the results of testing.

- It is impossible to guarantee that data entered is error free. Validation checks and verification checks help to reduce errors.

- Validation checks make sure that data entered is both sensible and possible.

- Verification tries to ensure that data entered is correct.

- Dry runs are paper-based runs of an algorithm or program.

- Trace tables allow a programmer to easily pinpoint where errors are, but can be extremely long and time-consuming to produce.

- Syntax errors occur when the programmer enters code that does not follow the rules of the programming language.

- Logic errors occur where the programmer writes code that does not perform as intended.

Exam-style questions

1   Describe what is meant by a library routine and suggest reasons why using such a routine is of benefit to a programmer.   (2 marks)

2   Seema wishes to design an algorithm using a flowchart. Discuss the possible benefits and drawbacks of using a flowchart to design her algorithm.   (2 marks)

3   Consider this algorithm:

```
value ← 0
nextValue ← 0
INPUT value
INPUT nextValue
WHILE nextValue != 0# != means not
   IF nextValue > value# note indentation
      value = nextValue
   ENDIF
   INPUT nextValue
ENDWHILE
OUTPUT value
```

Complete the following trace table using the input data 4, 3, 10, 1, 0, 15:   (5 marks)

value	nextValue	WHILE nextValue != 0	IF nextValue > value	OUTPUT value

4   Explain the difference between a logic error and a syntax error.   (2 marks)

5   Explain the difference between validation and verification.   (2 marks)

6   Why is it important to use test data? Use examples in your answer.   (4 marks)

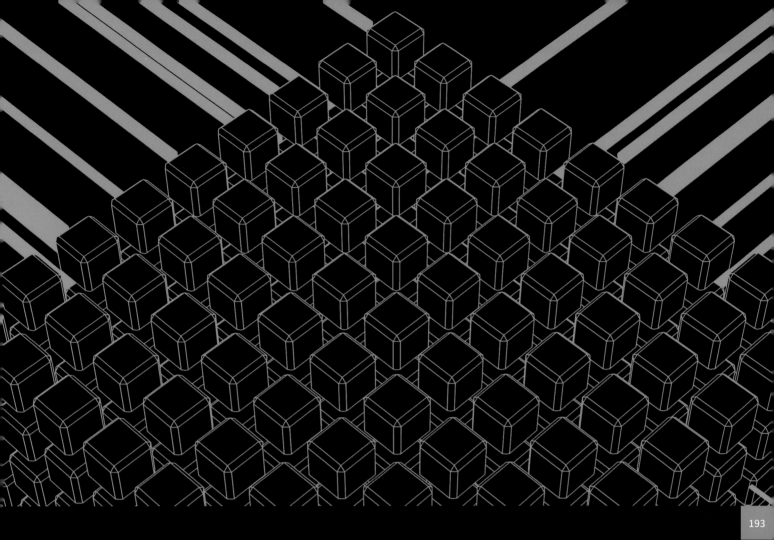

Chapter 14:
Databases

Learning objectives

By the end of this chapter you will:

- understand what is meant by a database
- know that a database can be paper-based or electronic
- understand what databases are used for
- understand what is meant by database structure, including tables, records and fields
- understand what is meant by a single table (flat file) database
- understand that different data types exist and how to choose a suitable data type for a field
- understand what is meant by a primary key and how to choose a suitable primary key
- understand what is meant by a query and how to perform a query-by-example
- understand that data in a database is only of use if it is reliable
- be able to explain the consequences of unreliable data in a database.

14.01 What is a database?

A database is a collection of **data** that is stored in a logical and organised manner. Databases are often electronic, but they do not have to be. Many databases are paper-based, for example a catalogue or a telephone directory. In fact, any collection of data can be called a database if the data is stored logically and in a structured format.

KEY TERM

Data – raw facts and figures.

Databases can be used in a number of ways, for example:

- Patient medical records held at a hospital are used by doctors and nurses to help treat patients.

- Search engines store data about websites, such as their name, web address and their content; users can quickly search for and find the information they are looking for.

- TV program listings contain the TV channels available, the programmes they are to show and their viewing time.

- Telephone directories contain the names, addresses and telephone numbers of people and businesses.

- Online shop databases store data about all the products the shop sells so that customers can browse for and order items.

- In schools, databases can store data about pupils such as their name, date of birth and address. They could store attendance registers. They could also be used by teachers to record classwork marks and exam results.

- A library stores each book's data, such as title, genre and author, so that someone can easily search for a book.

An electronic database is a database that is created and stored on a computer. In an electronic database a computer program can be used to quickly select the data that we require. Electronic databases are widely used because of the advantages they offer to the user (see Table 14.01).

Table 14.01

Advantage	Example
The data can easily be sorted in a specific way, for example alphabetically or from highest to lowest	A sort could be used to arrange products in an online shop by price, popularity or average customer review. It could also be used to arrange marks in a teacher's mark book by exam score
The data we need can be found quickly	In a library, it may take us time to find the book we want. If the library has an electronic database of books, we could search for the book and the database would tell us exactly where to find the book in the library

Also, we may not remember the name of the book, only the author. If we search for an author in the database we can see what books they have written and this may prompt our memory for the one we were looking for |

Advantage	Example
Data can be filtered to retrieve only the data we require	An online provider of television programs and movies would have a filter on their database. If we like science fiction movies we can just request, by selecting the Science Fiction category, to see those movies in the database
Data can easily be shared over the internet or using a portable storage device such as an external hard drive	A clothing retail chain, with a number of branches, may want stores to know the stock levels in a warehouse. The warehouse could share a database to show each branch the levels of stock left of the products that are sold. This way, the retail branches always know what clothing products are in stock
Data can be validated to make sure that data entered is possible, realistic and sensible	Validation could be used in an electronic database of patient records in a hospital. If there was no validation present on the patient's date of birth it could be entered as 1st January 2001, 01/01/2001, 01/01/01 or even 1/1/01. When a doctor wanted to search for patients born on 01/01/2001, it would only pick up records where the data had been entered in this way, giving a false figure. If we force the user to enter the data in the format DD/MM/YYYY then all the date-of-birth data would have to be entered in this way, making the database more reliable. This is more difficult to do with a paper-based system, in which rules can be suggested, but not enforced
A backup copy of the database can easily be made	A school could store a backup copy of all the students' records on a portable storage device. It could even keep this backup copy in fire-proof box. If the school were ever to suffer a network failure or even a fire and lose all the student records, they could use the backup copy to get the student data back again. A paper-based database can be copied but it might be very time consuming to copy, especially if the data runs to thousands of documents
It saves space compared to a paper database	A bank could store thousands of records in one electronic database, on a computer or portable storage device. A paper-based database would need a great number of filing cabinets or other storage methods to store thousands of records. This could take up a lot of valuable space in an office

Storage devices and validation are mentioned in Table 14.01. If you would like to learn more about storage devices, see Chapter 8. If you would like to learn more about validation, see Chapter 13.

14.02 Database structure

SYLLABUS CHECK

Define a single-table database from given data storage requirements.

Before creating a database there needs to be some consideration given to its structure. It must be decided what data it will hold and how much data needs to be stored. This will affect the size of the database and how much storage space it will need.

 KEY TERM

Table – a structure in which data is stored in a database.
Flat file database – a database whose records are stored in a single table.
Record – a collection of data about one single item in a database.
Field – one piece of data about an item in a database.

195

A **table** is the simplest structure in which to hold data. For example, the data in a contact list might be just names, phone numbers and birthdays.

Name	Phone number	Birthday
John	08881-764538	2nd October
Venkhat	08881-983726	13th June
Fatmia	08881-229220	21st May
Tanjung	08881-123987	27th September
Steffi	08881-445589	8th February

Figure 14.01 A paper-based database of a contact list

An electronic database is basically a digital filing system. Databases store data in tables. A database with a single table is called a **flat file database**. The tables are made up of **records** and **fields**. A record is a collection of data about one single item in a database. A field is one piece of data about an item in a database.

A record →

Student Name	Phone number	Birthday
John	08881-7645378	02/10
Venkhat	08881-983726	13/06
Fatima	08881-229220	21/05
Tanjung	08881-123987	27/09
Steffi	08881-445589	08/02

A field

Figure 14.02 A simple electronic database storing a contact list

TEST YOURSELF

Look at the example of the contact list database:

1 How many tables does it have?

2 Is it a flat file database?

3 How many records does it have?

4 How many fields does it have?

14.03 Data types

KEY TERM

Data type – the format of the data in a field.

A data type is a format that we can give to data in a field. When entering data into a database there we need to consider the appropriate **data type** for each field. The data type of a field will depend on the data that is being stored in that field. Various data types are shown in Table 14.02.

Table 14.02

Data type	Description	Example
Text (alphanumeric)	Any characters or symbols on a keyboard	Hello
Integer	A whole number that does not have any decimal places	100
Real	A number that does have decimal places	1.01
Date/time	Dates and times	01/01/2015 12:30
Boolean	Data that has only two possible values	Yes/no True/False

Consider the simple student database in Figure 14.03.

Student Name	Date of Birth	Attempts at test	Average Score	Re-sit?
Peter	07/08	3	8.6	No
Amy	28/02	2	9.5	No
Vikram	07/08	3	9.1	No
Seema	29/09	3	6.3	Yes
Amy	06/03	2	9.1	No

Figure 14.03

The database contains five fields. Each field requires a different data type.

Table 14.03

Field name	Data type
Student Name	Text
Date of Birth	Date/time
Attempts at test	Integer
Average Score	Real
Re-sit?	Boolean

It is very important to choose the correct data type for each field. If the wrong data type is chosen, data could be stored incorrectly. For example, in the student database, if the data type for the average score is specified as an integer, the scores will not be stored correctly. This is because only a whole number would be stored. Peter's score of 8.6 may be rounded up to 9 or truncated to 8. It could not be stored as 8.6 as that is not a whole number. The database would store an incorrect average score for Peter.

Data sometimes needs to be stored using a different data type than we might immediately think. For example, telephone numbers are often stored as text. In some countries, telephone numbers start with a 0. However, computers do not recognise 0s that occur at the beginning of integers, and would remove them from the data. The telephone number 01234 567890 stored as an integer would read 1234 567890. This means the telephone numbers would be missing their first digit and would be incorrect data. Specifying the data type as text overcomes this problem as the computer will now recognise the 0. Additionally, using a text data type allows spaces to be inserted in the phone numbers. This makes them easier to read.

To learn more about data types, see Chapter 11.

14.04 Primary keys

SYLLABUS CHECK

Choose a suitable primary key for a database table.

A table should have a field that will be a unique identifier for each record. This means that it will give each record a unique reference so that two records can be told apart. If two people in a database have the same name, a unique reference would be a way to tell the records apart. This unique identifier is called a **primary key.** It can also be known as a 'key field'.

 KEY TERM

Primary key – a unique identifier for each record in a database.

Index – a list of values or items.

In Figure 14.03, there are two students called Amy. Also, both Peter and Vikram have the same birthday. Therefore, neither the Student Name field nor the Date of Birth field would be suitable as a primary key, as not all the data in those fields are unique. Similarly, no unique data exists in any of the three remaining fields. As it stands, this database has no suitable field to use as a primary key as no field has unique data.

To overcome this problem we would add an extra field to the database. Each student could be given a unique ID number that could be used to tell his or her records apart. This field would be ideal as a primary key, since every item of data in that field can be unique.

Student ID	Student Name	Date of Birth	Attempts at test	Average Score	Re-sit?
1001	Peter	07/08	3	8.6	No
1002	Amy	28/02	2	9.5	No
1003	Vikram	07/08	3	9.1	No
1004	Seema	29/09	3	6.3	Yes
1005	Amy	06/03	2	9.1	No

Primary key

Figure 14.04 Database of students with a primary key added

Now each student can be uniquely identified. The key acts also as an **index** by which all records can be ordered and kept individual.

Consider this database about books:

Book title	Genre	Author	Reviewer's score	In print?	ISBN
Great Journeys	Travel	Kendo Takahashi	3.5	No	1863827662
Computer Science Projects	Computer Science	Sarah Lawrey	4.8	Yes	22990398272
Great Journeys	Astronomy	Jan Timmins	5.0	Yes	94837263728
Computing is Fun!	Computing	Sarah Lawrey	4.0	Yes	94220333723
100 Best Films ·	Film and TV	Dheeraj Saltani	3.5	No	83726372688

1 Can you identify the correct data type required for each field?
2 Is there a suitable field for a primary key or would an extra field need to be added?

14.05 Relational databases

An extension topic to the syllabus would be to look at databases that have more than one table.

A **relational database** is a database that has more than one table. The tables are related (linked) using their primary keys. For example, a veterinary practice might have a relational database with three tables, as shown in Table 14.04.

Table 14.04

Table	Primary key	Data stored
Owner	Owner Number	Data about each owner, such as their name and address. The Owner Number would be included in the Pet table to link the owner to the pet
Pet	Pet Number	Data about each pet, such as its name and breed. This table would also contain the Owner Number to link the owner to the pet
Appointment	Appointment Number	Data about each appointment, such as the time and date. The Pet Number would also appear in the table to link the pet to the appointment

KEY TERM

Relational database – a database that has several tables linked by primary key fields.

Foreign key – a primary key that appears in another table in a relational database.

The database structure would look like Figure 14.06.

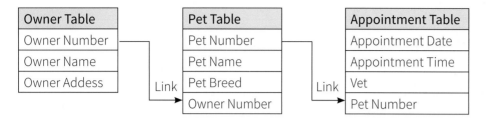

Figure 14.06 A relational database in a veterinary surgery

As the tables are linked, all relevant data can be seen easily:

- By looking up an owner, we could see which pets and appointments they have.
- By looking up a pet, we could see who their owner is and which appointments they have.
- By looking up an appointment, we could see which pet and owner the appointment is with.

When a primary key appears in another table it is called a **foreign key**.

Although a relational database is more complex in structure, it has several advantages over a flat file database.

Table 14.05

Advantage	Example
Data only needs to be entered once, but it can be used repeatedly within the database	An owner might have several pets. Each time a new pet's data is entered, the owner's data does not need to be re-entered. This is because the Owner Number in the Pet table provides a link to the owner's details. This reduces duplication of data and the size of the database. With a flat file database all the owner's data would have to be entered each time for every pet they have
Entering data only once reduces the chance of data errors	If we had to enter all the owner and pet data every time the pet had an appointment there is the possibility that on occasion the data would be entered incorrectly. With a flat file database this could lead to inconsistency in the data
If a data entry error has occurred the data only has to be corrected once	If the pet's name had been entered incorrectly, we would only need to correct the name in the Pets table. With a flat file database we would also have to correct the name in each record in the Appointments table where that pet appeared

14.06 Performing searches

Perform a query-by-example from given search criteria.

Databases can be very useful for searching through data. A search in a database is known as a **query**.

KEY TERM

Query – a method of searching a database.

SQL – a specialised programming language for maintaining databases and generating queries.

Query-by-example – a method of searching a database by stating the criteria to be searched.

When we search a database we use search criteria and we can do this by using **query-by-example**. In a query-by-example we choose each field we want to appear in the results and set any criteria we want to apply to that field.

There are a few items of data we need to include in our query-by-example, these are:

- The table
- The field
- The criteria
- Any sorting that we want to apply
- If we require the field to appear in the results or not.

We can structure this in a table type format to show what we want to perform as a search. For example, if we wanted to search our student database for those students who have taken less than three attempts at the test and have an average score of 9 or above. We want our results to only show the name of the student and no further data. Our query-by-example would look like this:

Table:	Students	Students	Students
Field:	Student Name	Attempts at test	Average Score
Sort:			
Criteria:		<3	=>9
Show:	✓	☐	☐

By placing 'less than 3' in the criteria for the number of attempts at the test and 'equal to or greater than 9' in the criteria, this will provide us with the students that meet the criteria requested. You will note that the only box ticked in the 'Show:' section is for Student Name. This is because the only field we wanted to see in our search result is the name of the student.

If we wanted to see students that have taken less than three attempts or had an average score of 9 or above we would change our query slightly to this:

Table:	Students	Students	Students
Field:	Student Name	Attempts at test	Average Score
Sort:			
Criteria:		<3	
			=>9
Show:	✓	☐	☐

You will note that the criteria for the average score now appears in the second criteria box. Each criteria that is placed in the first box will mean the results given must meet all of the criteria requested. If a criteria is placed in the second criteria box, this means that the results must meet either the first or the second criteria.

Many databases use a special-purpose programming language called **SQL** (Structured Query Language). SQL allows a database programmer to create queries very similar to writing a sentence. For example, this SQL query would search for 'Seema' in our student database:

SELECT * FROM Students WHERE Name = 'Seema'

Table 14.06

Keyword	Meaning	Description
SELECT	The command that is being performed	Records are being selected
FROM	Specifies the table that will be searched	In this query, the table is Students
WHERE	Specifies the field that we want to search for the criteria	In this query, the field is Name
= 'Seema'	The criterion that we are searching for	This query searches for 'Seema' in the Name field of the Students table

The criteria can be chosen using one or more of several operators, shown in Table 14.07.

Table 14.07

Operator	Description	Example
=	Equal to	Eye colour = brown
>	Greater than	Number in stock > 10
<	Less than	Number sold < 5
>=	Greater than or equal to	Height >= 1.5
<=	Less than or equal to	Average test score <= 5
AND	Combines two criteria	Eye colour = brown AND Height > 1.5
OR	Either one criterion or another	Eye colour = brown OR Eye colour = blue
NOT	Excluding this criterion	Eye colour NOT brown

Consider the student database we examined in Figure 14.04.

We could perform a search for all students who need to re-sit a test:

Table 14.08

Table	Students
Criterion	Re-sit? = 'Yes'

The equivalent SQL query would be:

SELECT * FROM Students WHERE Re-sit? = 'Yes'

TEST YOURSELF

1 Which student records would be returned if this search was performed?
2 Why would the remaining student records not be returned?

We could perform a search for all students whose average score is over 9:

Table 14.09

Table	Students
Criterion	Average Score > 9

The equivalent SQL query would be:

SQL – a specialised programming language for maintaining databases and generating queries SELECT * FROM Students WHERE Average Score > 9

TEST YOURSELF

1   Which student records would be returned if this search was performed?
2   Why would the remaining student records not be returned?

We could perform a search for all students whose average scores are over 5 and who attempted the test less than 3 times:

Table 14.10

Table	Students
Criteria	Average Score > 9 AND Attempts at test < 3

The equivalent SQL query would be:

SELECT * FROM Students WHERE Average Score > 9 AND Attempts at test < 3

TEST YOURSELF

1   Which student records would be returned if this search was performed?
2   Why would the remaining student records not be returned?
3   Using the student database in Figure 14.04, create an SQL query or a query table for each of the following searches:
   a   Students who have scored higher than 5 on average.
   b   Students who do not need to re-sit a test.
   c   Students who have scored less than 9 on average or those who have taken the test 3 times.
   d   Students who have scored more than 8 on average and taken the test less than 3 times, or those who have scored less than 9 on average and taken the test twice.
   There may be more than one possible way of creating a query for some searches.

14.07 Data validation

The data in a database is only useful if it is accurate and reliable. Any data that is entered incorrectly can cause query results to be incorrect and unreliable.

Consider the student database in Figure 14.04 once again. Suppose Peter's name had been incorrectly entered as Peta. If the teacher using the database used a query to search Peter's record, the search would return no results. This is because the name Peter does not exist in the database.

Similarly, if the re-sit field for Peter had been left blank (neither Yes nor No has been entered), then a query looking for those students who do not need to re-sit a test would not include Peter in its results. Peter may need to retake the test, but the teacher would not know.

Data validation is the process of automatically checking whether the data entered is possible, realistic and sensible. Validation does not make sure that the data is correct, incorrect data could still be entered that passes the validation. It eliminates the entering of data that is not realistic or sensible. This is done by making sure that the data entered follows certain rules. For example, in our student database, Vikram has an average score of 9.1. The validation on the Average Score field is that the number entered must be between 0 and 10. Suppose his score had been entered as 1.9. The data would be incorrect, but as far as the database is concerned, quite possible as it passes the validation.

To learn more about the ways in which data entered can be validated, see Chapter 13.

TEST YOURSELF

Inaccurate data in databases can have serious consequences.

1   What could happen in a hospital as a result of data in a database being unreliable?
2   What might be the consequences for an online shop whose products are in a database with inaccurate data?

Summary

- A database is a collection of data stored in a logical and ordered manner. Databases can be either paper-based or electronic.
- All databases have a structure that allows the data held within them to be stored in a logical and orderly manner.
- Data is stored in tables consisting of records and fields.
- A database with a single table is known as a flat file database. A database with multiple tables is known as a relational database.
- A record is a collection of data about one single item in a database.
- A field is one piece of data about an item in a database.
- Each database field must be given a data type.
- Tables need a primary key, which is a field that holds data that uniquely identifies a record.
- A search for data in a database is known as a 'query'.
- SQL is a programming language that is used to maintain databases and to create queries. A common method of searching a database is using query by example.
- Data held within a database is only of use if it is reliable. Unreliable data can lead to serious consequences for users.

Exam-style questions

1 Explain what a database is. (1 mark)

2 Describe two advantages of using an electronic database over a paper-based system. (2 marks)

3 Match the correct term with its definition: (5 marks)

Field	A structure in which data is stored in a database
Query	A unique identifier for a record
Record	A collection of data about one single item in a database
Table	One piece of data about an item in a database
Primary Key	A method used to search a database

4 Explain why it is important to give the correct data type to a field. (2 marks)

5 Bosire has a simple flat file database. Its table has two fields: name and telephone number.

   a Explain why neither field is suitable as a primary key. What field could be added to create a primary key? (2 marks)

   b Why might a user choose to create a flat file database rather than a relational database? (1 mark)

6 A database stores data in a table called Cars. The table structure includes fields called Colour, Engine Size and Number of Doors. Write an SQL query-by-example which searches for red or blue cars, with 5 doors and an engine size of more than 1600cc. (5 marks)

7 Why can unreliable data be of concern to a database user? (1 mark)

Answers

The sample answers and marks provided are for the exam-style questions at the end of each chapter and have been written by the author. The way marks are awarded in examination may be different.

Chapter 1 Data Representation

1 The stopwatch would show 02:38:59.

(1 mark for correct hours)
(1 mark for correct minutes)
(1 mark for correct seconds)
Total 3 marks

2 A byte is:
- A unit of data. (1 mark)
- Normally 8 bits. (1 mark)

Total 2 marks

3 In hexadecimal notation it would be: C1E (1 mark for each correct hex value)

Total 3 marks

4 Two answers accepted from:
- It is easier for humans to read than binary. (1 mark)
- It is a much shorter way of representing a byte or bytes of data. (1 mark)
- It is easier to debug than binary. (1 mark)

Total 2 marks

5 Two answers accepted from:
- Change the resolution of the image to a lower resolution. (1 mark)
- Use lossy compression to remove the redundant data from the image. (1 mark)

- Use lossless compression that will look for repeating patterns in the image. (1 mark)

(1 mark for each method)
(1 mark for explanation)
Total 4 marks

6 The most suitable file extensions are:

	.jpg	.mp4	.mp3	.csv
Storing holiday photos	✓			
Storing holiday videos		✓		
Storing a favourite song			✓	
Storing data to be imported into other files				✓

(1 mark per correct tick)
Total 4 marks

7 Two answers accepted from:
- Each character will take up a byte of data. (1 mark)
- Each character has an individual code that can be represented in binary. (1 mark)
- Capital letters, lower case letters, numbers and punctuation all have their own binary code. (1 mark)
- Each binary code can also be presented in hexadecimal. (1 mark)
- The computer will process the binary code and reference it to the character set used (ASCII) to see what letter is pressed. (1 mark)

Total 2 marks

8 Two answers accepted from:
- Increase the sampling rate of the recording. (1 mark)
- This means that each sample interval will be closer together. (1 mark)
- If the sample intervals are closer together the recording will be closer to the original track, improving the quality. (1 mark)
Total 2 marks

Chapter 2 Communication and Internet Technologies

1 • the rate at which the transfer of data occurs (1 mark)
- the number of bits that can be transmitted in a given period of time (1 mark)
- measured in bits per second (bps) or megabits per second (Mbps). (1 mark)
Total 3 marks

2 Two answers accepted from:
- Safer transmission as it is easier to accurately collate the bits together as they are sent one at a time. (1 mark)
- Reduced costs as only single wire needed. (1 mark)
- It can transmit over long distances. (1 mark)
- Simpler to implement than parallel transmission. (1 mark)
Total 2 marks

3
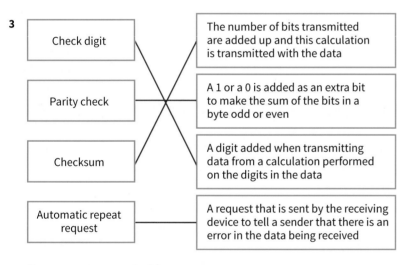

(1 mark per correct line)
Total 4 marks

4 Two answers accepted from:
- It detects a virus attack on a computer by scanning the computer. (1 mark)
- If a virus is found the software will remove it. (1 mark)
- It cannot prevent an attack from happening, only detect it once it has happened. (1 mark)
Total 2 marks

5 Two answers accepted from:
- Use a web browser to display the website. (1 mark)
- He will put the address (URL) of the website into the address bar of the browser. (1 mark)
- The URL is translated into the website's unique address and the browser downloads the content from the web server at that address. (1 mark)
Total 2 marks

6 Advantages of CSS:
- All pages can be easily and quickly updated with one change. (1 mark)
- The CSS can be used again for another website if the same format is needed. (1 mark)
Total 2 marks

7 Describe the difference between a static IP and a dynamic IP.
- A static IP address is a fixed address. (1 mark)
- A device will retain the same address even if it is disconnected and reconnected to the network. (1 mark)
- A dynamic IP address is an address that changes. (1 mark)
- A device will have the address for a limited period before it changes. This often happens when the device is disconnected and reconnected to a network, but it can happen at any time. (1 mark)

(1 mark for each definition)

(1 mark for explanation)

Total 4 marks

8 Cookies raise concern because:
- They can be used to track an internet user's activity. (1 mark)
- This data can then be sold to marketing companies so that a user can have specific adverts targeted at them. (1 mark)
- This can raise concern as it is possible to build up patterns about a person's internet use and possibly part of their identity. (1 mark)
- They can also be used to store sensitive information such as passwords. (1 mark)
- This means that the password can be automatically entered by the system at a later date when needed. (1 mark)
- This can raise concern as data is being held about our account information that could be stolen. (1 mark)

(1 mark for each point)

(1 mark for explanation)

(1 mark for each concern)

Total 6 marks

Chapter 3 Computer Architecture, Languages and Operating Systems

1 Stages of the fetch–execute cycle:

Step 1 – The CPU fetches the necessary data and instructions and stores them in its own internal memory locations. To fetch the instruction the CPU uses the address bus. The data is then moved to a special register that will decode the instruction. (1 mark)

Step 2 – The CPU decodes the instruction using an instruction set. (1 mark)

Step 3 – Once the CPU has decoded the instruction it executes the instruction. If any arithmetic calculations are needed, this will be carried out by the ALU. (1 mark)

Total 3 marks

2
- A register is an internal memory location within the CPU (1 mark)
- It temporarily holds data and instructions whilst they are being processed. (1 mark)

(1 mark per correct point)

Total 2 marks

3

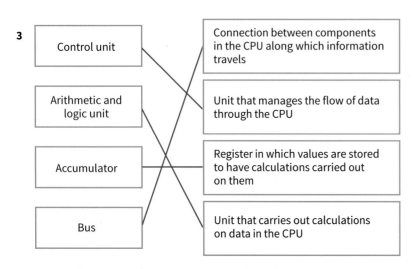

(1 mark per correct line)

Total 4 marks

4 Three answers accepted from:
- allows us to communicate with the hardware of a computer (1 mark)
- controls the peripheral devices in a system (1 mark)
- manages the transfer of programs into and out of memory (1 mark)
- divides the processing time between current applications that are running (1 mark)
- manages security software such as antivirus and firewalls (1 mark)
- manages file handling (1 mark)
- manages utility software. (1 mark)

Total 3 marks

5 Two answers accepted from:
- They are much easier to understand as they are closer to our native language. (1 mark)
- One line of code can do several things. (1 mark)
- Less knowledge is needed about the CPU to use a high-level language than a low-level language. (1 mark)
- They are mostly independent of any hardware they are run on. (1 mark)

Total 2 marks

6
- A compiler is a computer program that takes code written in a high-level language and translates it into machine code all in one go. (1 mark)
- An interpreter translates code line by line. (1 mark)

(1 mark per correct definition)

Total 2 marks

7 An assembler is a computer program that will take the basic instructions (mnemonics) used in assembly language and convert them into machine code so they can be processed by the computer. (1 mark)

8

Statement	True	False
Low-level languages are a computer's native language	✓	
Low-level languages need to be compiled before they can be processed		✓
Low-level languages are much easier for humans to understand		✓
In a low-level language one line of code will perform one task only	✓	

(1 mark per correct tick)

Total 4 marks

Chapter 4 Logic Gates

1 A logic gate controls the flow of electrical signals in a circuit. (1 mark)

Total 2 marks

2 **a** X = (*A AND B*) OR (NOT C) (3 marks)
b X = 0 (1 mark)
c X = 0 (1 mark)

Total 2 marks

3

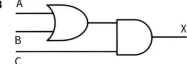

(1 mark per correct logic gate)

Total 2 marks

4

Input			Output
A	B	C	X
0	0	0	0
1	0	0	1
0	1	0	0
1	1	0	1
0	0	1	0
1	0	1	1
0	1	1	1
1	1	1	0

(1 mark for 2 correct values)
(2 marks for 4 correct values)
(3 marks for 7 correct values)
Total 3 marks

5 a Alarm = (*A AND B*) *NOT C*

(2 marks)

b

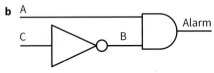

(1 mark per correct logic gate)
Total 2 marks

c

A	B	C	Alarm
0	1	0	0
1	1	0	1
0	0	1	0
1	0	1	0

1 mark for 2 correct values
2 marks for 4 correct values
Total 2 marks

Chapter 5 Input Devices

1 Two answers accepted from:
- touchscreen .... (1 mark)
- keyboard .... (1 mark)
- microphone. .... (1 mark)
- camera .... (1 mark)
- accelerometer .... (1 mark)

Total 2 marks

2 One answer accepted from:
- input data into a computer .... (1 mark)
- give a computer instructions. .... (1 mark)

Total 1 mark

3
- Manual input devices (e.g. keyboard, mouse, button) require the user to enter data/instructions. (1 mark)
- Automatic devices (e.g. sensors) input data without user interaction. (1 mark)

(1 mark per correct point)
Total 2 marks

4 Two answers accepted from:
- provide further information about a product or an offer (1 mark)
- provide a link to the business' website or a social media site (1 mark)
- provide a link to a promotional video. (1 mark)

Total 2 marks

5
- Captive touch screens. (1 mark)
- Use the natural electrical signals that we have in our bodies to detect when we are touching the screen. (1 mark)
- Resistive touch screens (1 mark)
- Have multiple layers with space in between. When slight pressure is applied to the screen the layers touch and the device recognises that we are touching the screen. (1 mark)

(1 mark for identification of type of touch screen: (captive/resistive)

(1 mark for each correct explanation)

Total 4 marks

6 An analogue-to-digital converter is also needed when inputting data because:
- computers use digital data (1 mark)
- microphones record analogue data (1 mark)
- the analogue data must be converted to digital before the computer can use it. (1 mark)

(1 mark per correct point)

Total 3 marks

7 Two answers accepted from:
- A photograph can be viewed immediately after it is taken, whereas with a film camera the film has to be processed. (1 mark)
- A digital photograph can be easily copied, unlike a film photograph which needs another copy developed from a negative. (1 mark)
- Digital photographs can be easily shared online, whereas a film photograph would need scanning first. (1 mark)
- Digital photographs can be easily edited, or retouched, unlike film photographs. (1 mark)

(1 mark for correct point)

(1 mark for explanation)

Total 4 marks

8 Two answers accepted from:
- Interactive whiteboards are large in size, which allows information displayed on them, such as text, images, graphs and charts. (1 mark)
- They can be seen by many people at the same time. (1 mark)
- The whiteboard also functions as an input device, which allows the trainer to annotate and add information, or draw diagrams to help illustrate points. (1 mark)
- The trainer can also control the computer without having to move away from the whiteboard. (1 mark)

Total 2 marks

9 A barcode works as follows:
- Barcodes are a series by black vertical bars with spaces (white vertical bars) between them. (1 mark)
- A barcode reader scans the barcode and translates it into a number. (1 mark)
- This number is usually a product number or code. (1 mark)
- The code can then be looked up in a database to find the rest of the product's data, such as its price or manufacturer. (1 mark)

(1 mark per correct point)

Total 4 marks

10 • A 3D scanner uses a laser to detect an object's geometry and size. (1 mark)
   • This data is input into a computer and recorded. (1 mark)
   • For example, film studios use 3D scanners to model actors' sizes and physical characteristics when (1 mark)
   producing animation. (1 mark per correct point)
   (1 mark for an example)
   Total 3 marks

Chapter 6 Sensors

1 A sensor is a type of input device that detects changes in the environment around it. (1 mark)

2 The following three sensors could be used:
   • A temperature sensor could monitor the heat in the nuclear plant and detect if it gets too high or too low. (1 mark)
   • A gas sensor could be used to detect the presence of any gases that could be hazardous in the (1 mark)
   nuclear plant.
   • A pressure sensor could be used to measure the flow of any liquids around the plant. (1 mark)
   (1 mark per correct point)
   Total 3 marks

3 Two drawbacks of using motion sensors in a security system could be:
   • If an alarm is set to sound when one sensor is triggered then the alarm may sound too easily and (1 mark)
   unnecessarily
   This is because something small such as a falling object or a rodent could trigger the alarm, but they (1 mark)
   may not be an intruder.
   • In this case an alarm could be set to sound if two or more sensors are triggered. (1 mark)
   • If the system used motion sensors that work by detecting heat, an intruder could use a heat (1 mark)
   protection suit to stop their body radiating heat.
   This would mean that the motion detector could not detect them.
   • In this case, creating a system that had more than one type of motion sensor, such as heat and (1 mark)
   microwave detectors, would mean that motion could be detected in two ways.
   (1 mark per correct point)
   (1 mark for explanation)
   Total 4 marks

4 Three answers accepted from:
   • A farmer could use moisture sensors to monitor the level of moisture in the soil. (1 mark)
   • This means that he can water the crops when the level of moisture gets too low. (1 mark)
   • This will stop the crops getting too dry. (1 mark)
   • He can also stop watering them if the moisture level gets too high, to stop the ground becoming waterlogged. (1 mark)
   • This means that the farmer can get the best crop possible by monitoring the level of moisture in the (1 mark)
   soil and keeping it consistent.
   Total 3 marks

5 • An infrared sensor detects infrared radiation that emits from a person or object. (1 mark)
   • These waves of radiation can trigger many different things such as a sensor in an alarm or change a (1 mark)
   channel on a television. (1 mark per correct point)
   Total 2 marks

212

6 When using a barcode scanner:
- A light shines on the barcode from the device. (1 mark)
- Light will then be reflected back to the device. (1 mark)
- The white areas of the code will reflect more light than the black areas. (1 mark)
- The scanner will then convert the light reflections and create a series of binary digits that can be (1 mark)
  read by a computer. (1 mark per correct point)

Total 4 marks

Chapter 7 Output Devices

1 Two answers accepted from:
- is a hardware device (peripheral) (1 mark)
- enables a user to output information (1 mark)
- allows a user to view the results of an input that has been processed. (1 mark)

Total 2 marks

2 LCD screens are more suited to portable devices because:
- LCD screens are much thinner in depth than CRTs, making them more portable. (1 mark)
- LCD screens use less energy than CRTs, increasing the battery life of a device. (1 mark)

(1 mark per correct point)

Total 2 marks

3 Two answers accepted from:
- RGB colours are dark ink/toner colours. (1 mark)
- Mixing dark ink/toner colours creates darker ink/toner colours, making it impossible to create light colours. (1 mark)
- They use CMYK that are light ink/toner colours. (1 mark)
- As they are light colours, they can be mixed to create other light colours and dark colours. (1 mark)

Total 2 marks

4 Two answers accepted from:
- It can produce high quality text outputs. (1 mark)
- It can quickly print many pages, making it suitable for essays and reports. (1 mark)
- They are cheap to run and can print double sided, making them suitable for students on a budget. (1 mark)

Total 2 marks

5 The resolution of a display:
- Is built up of thousands of tiny illuminated dots called pixels. (1 mark)
- Is the amount of pixels the display contains. (1 mark)
- The more pixels the display contains, the higher its resolution. (1 mark)

(1 mark per correct point)

Total 3 marks

6 Two answers accepted from:
- 3D printers allow quick production of small, individual items. (1 mark)
- A user at home can draw an object and print it out. (1 mark)
- This means that a user could create a replacement part for a broken item, a missing part for a model (1 mark)
  or a new protective case for a smartphone.
- Designs for many common items are now available for free on the internet, making replacing a broken (1 mark)
  or lost item a much simpler matter.

- However, at the moment 3D printers are expensive to buy. (1 mark)
- They also only print objects from certain materials such as plastic, making them unsuitable for (1 mark)
  producing items that require great strength.
- Over time 3D printing may become more common as the price of printers may fall and more designs (1 mark)
  become freely available. **Total 4 marks**

Chapter 8 Storage Devices

1 • Primary storage is a computer's internal storage, such as RAM and ROM. (1 mark)
- Secondary storage is storage external to a computer, such as a hard disk drive or compact disk. (1 mark)
  (1 mark per correct definition)
  Total 2 marks

2 Three answers accepted from:
- RAM is volatile; ROM is non-volatile. (1 mark)
- RAM is temporary; ROM is (semi)permanent. (1 mark)
- RAM tends to be much greater in capacity than ROM. (1 mark)
- RAM holds data and programs for processing; ROM holds firmware and bootstraps. (1 mark)
  Total 3 marks

3 How a hard disk drive reads and writes data:
- Hard disk drives use electromagnets attached to read/write heads and magnetic fields to manipulate (1 mark)
  tiny magnetic dots of data.
- Data is stored in tracks on disks (platters) that are attached to a spindle. (1 mark)
- As the spindle turns, the platters rotate. (1 mark)
- Data is read/written as the dots in the tracks move under a read/write head. (1 mark)
  (1 mark per correct point)
  Total 4 marks

4 Two answers accepted from:
- Optical disk drives use a laser to scan tracks on optical disks. (1 mark)
- Blu-ray devices use higher frequency lasers than compact disk devices. (1 mark)
- The higher the frequency of the laser, the more closely the data can be packed together on the tracks. (1 mark)
- More data can be stored in an equivalent space. (1 mark)
  Total 2 marks

5 Two answers accepted from:
- An optical medium such as CD ROM or DVD ROM would be ideal as they are high in capacity, read only, (1 mark)
  portable and cheap to buy and transport.
- The catalogue may need a large file size so it is not suitable to email. (1 mark)
- The catalogue needs to be read-only to avoid customers changing details. (1 mark)
- The medium must be portable and cheap to produce for a large audience. (1 mark)
  Total 2 marks

6 Calculation could show: (1 mark)

$$4 \text{ inches} \times 1 \text{ inch} = 4 \text{ square inches}$$
$$600 \text{ dpi} \times 4 \text{ square inches} = 2400 \text{ pixels}$$
$$2400 \text{ pixels} \times 16 \text{ bits} = 38\,400 \text{ bits}$$
$$38\,400 \text{ bits} \div 8 = 4800 \text{ bytes}$$
$$800 \text{ bytes} \div 1024 = 4.69 \text{ kilobytes}$$

214

7 Two answers accepted from:
- Data is stored serially on magnetic tape. (1 mark)
- If the data required is near the point at which the tape starts being read, then the data will be quickly found and transferred. (1 mark)
- If the data is far away from that point, the tape has to loop around to the correct place first, slowing down the transfer. (1 mark)

Total 2 marks

8 Two answers accepted from:
- It is generally more expensive to buy. (1 mark)
- It is normally smaller in capacity than hard disk drives. (1 mark)

(1 mark per correct point)

Total 2 marks

Chapter 9 Security

1
- The more accurate and complete data is, the more valuable it is. (1 mark)
- If data is lost, corrupted or accidentally changed, it becomes less accurate and complete and loses value. (1 mark)

(1 mark per correct point)

Total 2 marks

2 An automatic backup:
- is where a computer makes a backup made without user intervention (1 mark)
- is where the computer automatically creates a backup at a scheduled time and date. (1 mark)

(1 mark per correct point)

Total 2 marks

3 Four answers accepted from:
- Phishing uses email that pretends to come from a person or organisation the user is familiar with. (1 mark)
- The email asks the user to confirm account details by clicking on a link. (1 mark)
- If clicked, the link directs the user to a fake website that looks like the organisation's real site, where they can be tricked into giving up personal data. (1 mark)
- Pharming also uses fake websites to try to gain access to personal data. (1 mark)
- When a user tries to visit a genuine site they are instead directed to a fake site. (1 mark)
- If the user enters personal data on the fake site the data is stolen and passed to criminals. (1 mark)

Total 4 marks

4 Answers could include:
- Denial of service attacks occur when malware on a computer instructs the computer to send a high volume of requests to a server. (1 mark)
- Anti-virus software detects and removes malware from computers, removing the cause of the attack. (1 mark)

(1 mark per correct point)

Total 2 marks

5 Four answers accepted from:
- Malware is software that is designed to disrupt or modify a computer system. (1 mark)
- It is usually accidentally downloaded from email attachments, websites and USB sticks. (1 mark)
- Anti-virus software detects and removes malware from a computer, helping to keep the computer safe. (1 mark)

- Computers communicate by sending messages. Most messages a computer sends are authorised. (1 mark)
- Some messages are created by malware or hackers. These messages are unauthorised messages. (1 mark)
- Firewalls monitor communications to prevent unauthorised messages from being sent, helping to keep the computer safe. (1 mark)

Total 4 marks

6 Two answers accepted from:
- A proxy server is a computer that sits between a network server and the internet. (1 mark)
- The proxy server directs traffic away from the main server by examining the traffic. (1 mark)
- If the traffic is authorised it is forwarded to the network server; if not, the traffic is kept away from the network server, keeping it and the data on it safe. (1 mark)

Total 2 marks

7 Four answers accepted from:
- Encryption converts data into a form that cannot be understood by anyone other than an authorised user. (1 mark)
- Encryption works by using a key. (1 mark)
- Symmetric encryption uses the same key to encrypt and decrypt data. (1 mark)
- Asymmetric encryption uses two separate keys which work as a pair. (1 mark)
- The first key is used to encrypt the data. (1 mark)
- The second key is used to decrypt the data. (1 mark)

Total 4 marks

8 Two answers accepted from:
- A protocol is a set of rules that governs communications between computers. (1 mark)
- Some protocols, such as secure socket layer, use asymmetric encryption to create a secure link between one computer and another. (1 mark)
- This means that data can be safely transmitted between computers as anyone without the encryption keys cannot read the data. (1 mark)

Chapter 10 Ethics

1 Computer ethics refers to acts of using a computer in a rightful or wrongful manner. There is not an agreed set of ethics as what one person thinks is right another may think is wrong. (2 marks)

2 Two answers accepted from:
- because the use of computers needs to be governed to control how they are used for our safety (1 mark)
- to stop the misuse of computers when communicating (1 mark)
- to stop theft of other people's work or details using the internet. (1 mark)

Total 2 marks

3 It would be free software. (1 mark)

4
- Malware is often disguised as an email attachment, or as a link included within an email. (1 mark)
- When a user downloads the email attachment, or clicks on a link, the malware is installed on the user's computer without their knowledge. (1 mark)

(1 mark per correct point)

Total 2 marks

5 Answers could include:
- Images featured on a commercial website may well have been commissioned and paid for by the company. (1 mark)
- The company will own the copyright to those images, which means we cannot use those images without the company's permission. (1 mark)

(1 mark per correct point)

Total 2 marks

Chapter 11 Programming Concepts

1
- A variable is a named location in memory that holds data that may change during the running of a program, for example, the value of a running total. (1 mark)
- A constant is a named location in memory that holds data that does not change, for example, the value of pi. (1 mark)

(1 mark per correct point)

Total 2 marks

2 Suitable data types would be:
- **a** String (1 mark)
- **b** Integer (1 mark)
- **c** Character (1 mark)
- **d** Integer/float (depending if the score will be a wholeor a decimal number) (1 mark)

(1 mark per correct data type)

Total 4 marks

3 a Explanations could include the following steps:
1. Input a mark. (1 mark)
2. Add 1 to a count of the number of marks. (1 mark)
3. Add the mark to the total. (1 mark)
4. When there are no more marks, divide the total by the count of how many marks. (1 mark)
5. Output the answer. (1 mark)

or
1. Input the number of marks. (1 mark)
2. Until the number in Step 1 is reached (1 mark)
2. a Input a mark. (1 mark)
2. b Add it to a total. (1 mark)
3. Loop back to step 2. (1 mark)
4. Divide the total by the number of marks. (1 mark)
5. Output the answer. (1 mark)

(1 mark per correct step in the explanation)

Total 5 marks

b
- A condition loop would be used. (1 mark)
- A condition loop continues until a condition is met. In this example the condition to be met is 'no more marks to be entered'. The loop will continue until there are no more marks. (1 mark)

Total 2 marks

4 Sequence is important because if the sequence of instructions is incorrect the program will not function as intended. For example, if a program to calculate average scores works out the average before all scores have been input the average will be incorrect. (1 mark)

5 A programmer would use an array because:
- An array stores many data values under one name. (1 mark)
- Using an array means a programmer does not have to use many variables to hold data. (1 mark)

(1 mark per correct point)

Total 2 marks

6 A solution could be:

```
examscores ← []
FOR count ← 0 TO 14:
    PRINT "Type in a score"
    examscores[count] ← USERINPUT
NEXT count
```

(1 mark for initialising array)
(1 mark for correct loop start)
(1 mark for correct input into array)
(1 mark for correct loop end)
Total 4 marks

7 The two main things that we need to do are:
- state the array's name
- state the array's size.

(1 mark)
(1 mark)
(1 mark per correct point)
Total 2 marks

Chapter 12 Pseudocode and Flowcharts

1 Comments should be used because:
- They explain what a particular line or section of pseudocode is for or does.
- They help other programmers to understand our code.

(1 mark)
(1 mark)
(1 mark per correct point)
Total 2 marks

2 Flowcharts are a useful design tool because:
- They are a diagrammatical method of viewing an algorithm or program.
- They show a visual representation of a problem, which can help a programmer to more easily understand the logic of it.

(1 mark)
(1 mark)
(1 mark per correct point)
Total 2 marks

3 The symbol used to represent a decision in a flowchart is a diamond.

(1 mark)

4 Allow variations on:

```
PRINT "Enter the length of side 1 of the triangle"
side1 ←USERINPUT
PRINT "Enter the length of side 2 of the triangle"
side2 ←USERINPUT
PRINT "Enter the length of side 3 of the triangle"
Side3 ←USERINPUT
PRINT "Do you want to know the area or the perimeter of the triangle?"
answer ← USERINPUT
IF answer = "area" THEN
    s = (side1 + side2 + side3)/2
    result = √(s*(s - side1)*(s - side2)*(s - side3))
    PRINT "Area is ", area
ELSE
    result = (side1 + side2 + side3)
    PRINT "Perimeter is ", perimeter
ENDIF
```

(1 mark for input of sides)
(1 mark for correct use of selection)
(1 mark for correct calculation of area)
(1 mark for correct calculation of perimeter)
(1 mark for output of each result)
Total 5 marks

5 Allow variations on the following flowchart:

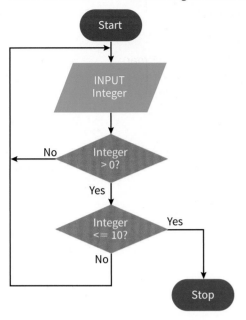

(1 mark for correct input)
(1 mark for decision on >0)
(1 mark for decision on <=10)
(1 mark for correct loop(s))
Total 4 marks

6 Allow variations on the following flowchart:

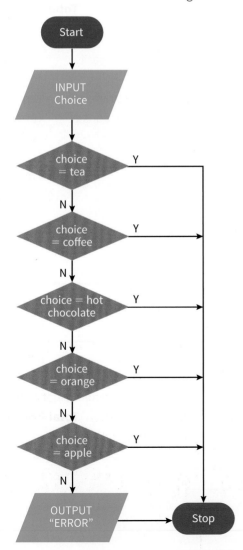

(1 mark for correct input)
(1 mark for correct case decisions (as a whole))
(1 ark for error output)
(1 mark for correct loop(s))
Total 4 marks

7 Three answers accepted from:
- Pseudocode and flowcharts are methods of describing how a program works. (1 mark)
- Pseudocode is a list of instructions, set out like a programming language, whereas a flowchart is a (1 mark) diagrammatical representation of the program.
- Both methods allow other programmers to easily understand how a program works. (1 mark)
- Flowcharts take a long time to produce and any changes to the algorithm will mean sections of the (1 mark) flowchart have to be redrawn.
- Pseudocode is quick to write and quick to amend. (1 mark)
- Amy is designing a very large program. She would be better off using pseudocode because creating a (1 mark) flowchart for such a large program would take her far longer to produce a design. **Total 3 marks**

Chapter 13 Algorithm Design and Problem-solving

1 Two answers accepted from:
- A library routine is a small, commonly used program or subroutine that can be used in another program, ((1 mark) for example a routine to generate random numbers.
- Library routines simplify a program because the code for them does not have to be written by the ((1 mark) programmer, seeing as it already exists.
- The programmer knows the code works, because it has already tested and used by other programmers. (1 mark) **Total 2 marks**

2 Two answers accepted from:
- In a flowchart the sequence of steps in the algorithm can easily be seen and paths through it can easily (1 mark) be traced.
- Using diagrams often makes it easier for other programmers to understand the logic of the program. (1 mark)
- However, flowcharts can take a long time to produce and changes to an algorithm will mean sections of (1 mark) the flowchart will have to be redrawn, which can take a long time.
- Long flowcharts can be complicated and hard to follow. (1 mark) **Total 2 marks**

3 Completed trace table:

value	nextValue	WHILE nextValue != 0	IF nextValue > value	OUTPUT value
0				
	0			
4				
	3			
		TRUE		
			FALSE	
	10			
		TRUE		
			TRUE	
10				
	1			
		TRUE		
			FALSE	
	0			
		FALSE		
				10

(1 mark per correct column in the table)
Total 5 marks

4
- A logic error is a coding error that causes a program to do something it should not, such as incorrectly calculating a result. (1 mark)
- A syntax error is an error that occurs when the written code does not follow the rules of the programming language, for example not using quotation marks to assign a value to a string. (1 mark) (1 mark per correct definition)

Total 2 marks

5
- Validation is a check made on entered data to attempt to reduce errors. Validation checks make sure data entered is both sensible and possible. (1 mark)
- Verification is a check made on entered data to attempt to reduce errors. Verification checks try to make sure the data entered is accurate. (1 mark) (1 mark per correct definition)

Total 2 marks

6 Four answers accepted from:
- Test data is important to ensure that a program works correctly. Test data is used to test that a program works and does what it is supposed to do. (1 mark)
- Test data can be normal data, extreme data or invalid data. (1 mark)
- Normal data is data that the program is expected to use. (1 mark)
- Extreme data is normal data at the boundaries of what is expected to be used. (1 mark)
- Invalid data is data that should not be accepted. (1 mark)
- For example, a teacher enters test scores into a program. The scores are out of 100. Normal data would be any score in the range 0 to 100. Extreme data would be data at the boundaries of the range, for example, 0, 1, 99 and 100. Invalid data would be any number below 0 or above 100. (1 mark)

Total 4 marks

Chapter 14 Databases

1 A database is a collection of logically organised data. (1 mark)

2 Two answers accepted from:
- Data can be sorted, for example students' marks could be sorted from highest to lowest. (1 mark)
- Data can be found much quicker as a computer can rapidly process data. (1 mark)
- Data can easily be filtered, as the computer can quickly remove non-matching data from a search. (1 mark)
- Data can easily be shared. (1 mark)
- Data can be backed-up as digital files. (1 mark)
- Data can be validated to help make sure it is sensible. (1 mark)
- Electronic databases on computers use less space than paper-based systems using filing cabinets. (1 mark)

Total 2 marks

3 The correct terms and definitions are:

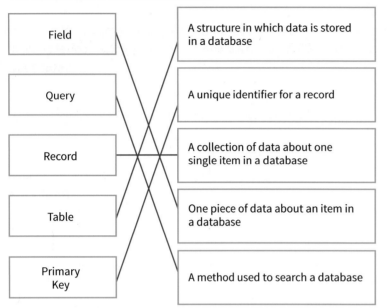

(1 mark per correct line)
Total 5 marks

Matching boxes:
- Field → One piece of data about an item in a database
- Query → A method used to search a database
- Record → A collection of data about one single item in a database
- Table → A structure in which data is stored in a database
- Primary Key → A unique identifier for a record

4 It is important to give the correct data type to a field because, if the wrong data type is chosen, data could be stored incorrectly. For example, if real number data is stored as integers the data would be rounded up or down and the data would be incorrect. (2 marks)

5 a Two answers accepted from:
- ○ Data in a primary key must be unique for each record. (1 mark)
- ○ More than one record could have the same data in the name field, as some people might have the same name. (1 mark)
- ○ More than one record could have the same data in the telephone number field, as some people might share a telephone number. (1 mark)
- ○ A field with a unique number for each record, such as Person ID, could be added for use as a primary key. (1 mark)

Total 2 marks

b A user might create a flat file database rather than a relational database if the database has only a small number of fields and very little (if any) duplicated data. (1 mark)

6 SELECT * FROM Cars WHERE Colour = 'red'
OR Colour = 'blue' AND doors = 5
AND engine size > 1600

(1 mark for correct select from statement) (1 mark for WHERE)
(1 mark for OR on correct colours)
(1 mark for AND on correct doors)
(1 mark for AND on correct engine size)
Total 5 marks

7 Unreliable data may be of concern to a database user because it means a user will get incorrect data when performing a search. (1 mark)

Index

224